Experiencing America: Through the Eyes of Visiting Fulbright Scholars

Stories of Foreign Fulbrighters in the United States

by

Editors: Zeeshan-ul-hassan Usmani and Omer Idrees

Bloomington, IN  Milton Keynes, UK
authorHOUSE

AuthorHouse™
1663 Liberty Drive, Suite 200
Bloomington, IN 47403
www.authorhouse.com
Phone: 1-800-839-8640

AuthorHouse™ *UK Ltd.*
500 Avebury Boulevard
Central Milton Keynes, MK9 2BE
www.authorhouse.co.uk
Phone: 08001974150

© 2006 Editors: Zeeshan-ul-hassan Usmani and Omer Idrees. All rights reserved.

No part of this book may be reproduced, stored in a retrieval system, or transmitted by any means without the written permission of the author.

First published by AuthorHouse 6/22/2006

ISBN: 1-4259-3645-8 (sc)

Library of Congress Control Number: 2006904412

Printed in the United States of America
Bloomington, Indiana

This book is printed on acid-free paper.

"The contents of this book have not been authorized by the Department of State or the Institute of International Education, and the views and opinions of authors expressed herein do not necessarily state or reflect those of the United States Government, the Fulbright Program, or IIE. These organizations do not assume any legal liability or responsibility for the accuracy, completeness, or usefulness of any information contained herein."

Binish Bhagwanee
Who Loves Pizza, Chocolates
and Me
~**Zeeshan-ul-hassan Usmani**

For my 'AMMI' and
My very own 'Jia'
~**Omer Idrees**

Thank You, Shukria (Urdu), Nga peno (Nufi), Spasibo (Russian), Webaare (Runyankole), Danke (German), Xie Xie (Mandarin), Terima Kasih (Malay), Bedankt (Dutch), Grazie (Italian), Shukran (Arabic)

In the name of Allah, the Most Beneficent and the Most Merciful; to Him is due all praise. We thank Him for giving us the ability to compile and put this book together.

"I would maintain that thanks are the highest form of thought, and that gratitude is happiness doubled by wonder."

~G. K. Chesterton

There are practically hundreds of people, who helped me to explore, understand and experience the United States and make my stay unforgettable There are some more important than others, not because of their education or social status, but because they helped me at right time, at the right place and with the right kind of guidance.

First and foremost, I want to extend our heartiest gratitude to Fulbright program, which makes it possible to come here. My IIE contact persons, David N. Hadley and Christina Holdvogt who are always there to respond my never-ending series of questions.

I would like to thank my co-editor Omer Idrees and my guest writers of Preface, Introduction and Forewords, and all those who contributed their experiences to this book and have made this work possible.

Last but not least I would like to thank my academic advisor Ronaldo Menezes and my beloved professor William D. Shoaff, who taught me how to write, study and work.

Thank you very much, all of you

Zeeshan-ul-hassan Usmani

Thank you, in contributor's languages

Editor's Note

Edward A. Murphy said, "If there's more than one way to do a job, and one of those ways will result in disaster, then somebody will do it that way". The generalized and widely known form of this law is ""Anything that can go wrong will go wrong".

We have tried to present the collection of essays in their true form as they were intended by the authors. However, in the process of editing the essays, Murphy's Law may have prevailed in some way and we may have unintentionally, hopefully insignificantly, altered some of the true form of the essays as they were intended by the authors.

In the event that the contributions have been significantly altered, either in form or purpose, we would like to place the blame on Murphy's Law.

In conclusion, we invite any comments, feedback or suggestions that you, the reader, may have.

Sincerely,

Editors

zeeshan_ul_hassan@yahoo.com
omer.idrees@gmail.com

Foreword

These stories of foreign Fulbrighter in the United States, "Experiencing America: Through the Eyes of Visiting Fulbright Scholars" gives the reader a firsthand account of the value of the international education exchange program. Each story is unique and personal, describing different impressions and values. Winnie Tarinyeba of Uganda felt her stay in the US gave her a new and important role in life. "The time that I have spent in the US has also enabled me to be an ambassador for my country. I have learned about other cultures and also helped others learn about my own country and its cultures."

Another Fulbrighter, Lynette J. Chua of Malaysia, valued her experience from a different viewpoint. "Perhaps 10 years ago, I was less mature and could not articulate why I did not find 'us' fundamentally different from 'them.' The answer, which I have now discovered, is that 'we' share an important similarity with 'them' and the similarity is love."

Russia's Marina Lukanina truly understood what Senator Fulbright had in mind for his scholars: "Fulbright is definitely helping me live my dream—to study and expand my knowledge, to acquire the invaluable experience of meeting and communicating with lots of different people. Fulbright provides significant positive influence on a person's development by giving him a chance to celebrate his difference. We will make future generations more perceptive and flexible. They will come to understand the necessity to learn and respect the differences in our diverse and fast-moving world."

I couldn't have said it better myself. These stories are very diverse, full of thoughtful descriptions of mental growth, some painful and others filled with joy. They are one of the best ways of understanding the value of international education exchange.

Harriet Mayor Fulbright
March 6, 2006

Preface

While all of us involved in the Fulbright program recognize that the Fulbright program exists to provide educational and cultural exchanges between the people of the U.S. and the people of other countries around the world, we may sometimes not realize in what varied ways this plays out for real individual grantees. It is very easy to focus on the broad goals of the program a whole, forgetting that each and every Fulbright recipient experiences the program in a series of insights and experiences unique to him or her.

Receiving a Fulbright scholarship is a great source of pride. It can also be a source of wonder, trepidation about moving far away from home and a known culture, anxiety about the new environment, unexpected joy, mountains of work, intense learning, new habits, new professional concepts, frustration, home sickness, new ideas about people and life, and new friends. The contributors to this volume, very real Fulbright student grantees, have been incredibly generous in sharing their experiences with the rest of us. They have shared their honest perceptions before coming to the U.S. and the experiences and thought processes that helped to change or intensify these ideas. In the process they relate very real adventures that are insightful, heartwarming, poignant, and sometimes funny. Their stories are sometimes distressing, but always insightful about how these very bright students see the U.S. and its people.

The stories shared in this book are especially useful for those considering coming to the U.S. to study. While U.S. schools and Education USA staff can repeat unlimited times that people in the U.S. are almost all warm and friendly to students from other countries, there is no substitute for hearing the stories of real students from countries outside the U.S. Each story also reinforces the reality that no one has an absolutely smooth experience, but that with imagination, patience, and a sense of humor, everyday obstacles can be overcome. The overwhelming message of each of the contributors is that their experience was, on the whole, very positive.

Every person interested in or involved with the Fulbright program should read this book. It helps to restore perspective about the experiences of real grantees. It provides excellent examples of what happens after students receive their grant and arrive in the U.S. Too often official reports focus on academic accomplishments, but this book relates stories about all aspects of life in the U.S. Readers may not agree with all of the writers' conclusions, but they will learn a lot about how those from outside the U.S. experience us.

There is also a cautionary tale here for those selecting Fulbrighters. Many people ask me what we look for when we select Fulbrighters. Of course we look for academic strength, good test scores, signs of leadership, and good references, but we also look for a special spark that is very hard to define, but that sets them apart from the rest. Zeeshan was obviously brilliant in his field, but not nearly as sophisticated or as polished as many of the more elite candidates against whom he competed. There was something special about him, however, and our panel selected him over hundreds of others because we believed in him and knew he would represent Pakistan well as a Fulbrighter and gain a lot from the experience. He has gone way beyond our expectations in his academic activities (he is delivering a paper at an academic conference, quite a coup for a Masters student) and in writing this book. His own experience demonstrates that special spark that just needs an opportunity to develop. .

Zeeshan-ul-hassan and his colleagues are to be commended for putting together this book. At a time in their lives that they are swamped with school work and enjoying their own adventures, they have chosen to share their experiences with others in writing so that others can profit by what they have learned. By doing this, they exemplify the special qualities of Fulbrighters to excel in academics and to share their experiences with other. I think the reader will find that all of these students are a credit to their own countries and to the Fulbright program.

Grace Clark, PhD.
Executive Director
United States Educational Foundation in Pakistan

Table of Contents

1. Forewords xi
   Harriet Mayor Fulbright

2. Preface xiii
   Dr. Grace Clark

3. Introduction xix
   Eric S. Howard

4. New York - The Big Apple Seen From its Very Core 1
   Alessandra Seggi – Italy

5. From Makerere to Stanford: The Experience of a Fulbright Scholar 19
   Winnie Tarinyeba - Uganda

6. Five Definitions of America – My Fulbright Journey 33
   Zeeshan-ul-hassan Usmani – Pakistan

7. From "Criminal" to Fulbrighter : in the land of Spartans 47
   Raymund Espinosa Narag – Philippines

8. It's Fun to Live Your Dream 57
   Marina Lukanina – Russia

9. The Odyssey of a Fulbrighter 69
   Louis-Marie Ngamassi Tchouakeu – Cameroon

10. Fulbright Experience of Love, Self-understanding and Self-emancipation 97
    Lynette J. Chua – Malaysia

11. Get back to where you now belong 109
    Katja Ziehmayer – Austria

12.	My Second Life..	123
	Anouk Bachman – Netherlands	
13.	The Contributors	139
14.	The Editors...	145

Introduction

Fresh flames spring up in the fireplace after I place a birch log on the embers of last night's fire, and the heat starts to warm the living room in this predawn hour. I have been up several times in the night to tend this fire and the one in the woodstove. They are the sole source of heat in this 160 year old New Hampshire farmhouse.

This land was settled shortly before the Civil War – in the 1840s and 1850s. A young entrepreneur dug the cellar hole by hand. The foundation stones were laid dry, without mortar, with stones found nearby. Similarly, the house was framed and built with timbers from the surrounding forest.

Since then, seasons have come and gone. There were freezes and thaws, flowers bloomed and leaves fell. The house settled on its foundation; the kids' marbles now always roll to one corner of the living room. The house had renovations and modifications, but the basic structure remained the same, and every morning – including today – the sun rises in the east over the nearby mountain.

The surrounding landscape, however, changed. Trees were harvested; forests were replaced by crops and pastures. Rocks were removed from fields and piled along the property line, making the famous stone walls of New England. And then, around the time of another war – World War II – most of the farms were abandoned. The economy changed, and better farmland was available out west. Neighboring houses and sheds rotted and collapsed. This particular home remains – the last house on the road, surrounded by thousands of acres of forest and conservation lands.

Over the years, the white clapboard structure has housed several families, and numerous guests have passed through it. Innumerable visitors have parked out front, be it to go for a walk in the woods or to hunt deer, moose, or turkeys to feed their families. A man from town comes regularly to collect wood to heat his house, and in exchange he cuts and splits wood for the fires in our house.

Why do I tell this story? How does it relate to a collection of essays by Fulbright scholars who have come to the United States to study and conduct research?

This story illustrates some of the interesting aspects of Fulbright – a unique, prestigious international exchange program. I am now the steward of this 1850's house, and I as a Fulbright scholar myself, I am also one of many stewards of a program that was begun by J. William Fulbright.

About a century after this house was conceived and around the time that the surrounding structures were abandoned, a young policy entrepreneur was elected by the citizens of Arkansas to represent them in Washington, DC. Shortly thereafter – in 1946 to be exact – it was he who laid the foundation and conceived the framework for a program which today shares his name: Fulbright.

In the intervening years, there have been political freezes and thaws, policy ideas have bloomed and withered away, but the program which Senator Fulbright conceived still exists today. The program remains strong, even as other programs have been abandoned – rotting from neglect or formally destroyed. In a world where information flows instantaneously but cultural understanding often ends at a national boarder, today's Fulbright program may be more important now than ever before.

Yes, there have been some changes to the program; it has evolved over the past sixty years. The authorizing legislation has been amended, new countries have been added, and every year there are small administrative changes. Nevertheless, the basic framework, the structure and goals have remained the same: increase international understanding by facilitating international exchanges of citizens.

> "The purpose of this Act is to enable the Government of the United States to increase mutual understanding between the people of the United States and the people of other countries by means of educational and cultural exchange: to strengthen the ties which unite us with other nations by demonstrating the educational and cultural interests, developments, and achievements of the people of the United States and other nations, and the contributions being made toward a peaceful and more fruitful life for people throughout the world; to promote international cooperation for educational and cultural advancement; and thus to assist in the development of friendly, sympathetic, and peaceful relations between the United States and the other countries of the world."
> (Fulbright-Hayes Act of 1961)

Since its establishment, nearly 300,000 people have been "Fulbright Scholars." Hundreds of thousands of others have served as local hosts to these visitors, helping them adapt to a new culture, providing space for research and scholarship, and building bridges between the different societies. In turn, these scholars and their hosts have influenced the entire world, through their teachings, their research, and their discoveries.

This year (2006) is the 60th Anniversary of the Fulbright Exchange Program, and a few of their stories have been gathered for this collection of essays. All of the contributors are grantees who came to the United States from other countries, some for the first time. The stories of these citizen ambassadors may be humorous or heart-wrenching, but they are all true.

Even if they are not yet aware of it, these grantees and the thousands of others who are awarded Fulbright grant this year have all have been welcomed into a program established by Senator Fulbright in 1946. We are all part of the Global Fulbright Network.

Fulbright ties are important because humans are not a solitary species. We live and work in communities. Scholars do not work in isolation, and scholarship is not static. And that is one of the beauties of the Fulbright program. It makes it possible for individuals to expand our personal and professional networks – to meet and interact with people in other countries and cultures, people that we would normally never meet.

For alumni of the program, that aspect of the Fulbright experience can continue. Fulbright grantees live and work on every continent, in every country, and so we will always have opportunities to interact with interesting people – people in our own academic disciplines or in others. This part of our learning and teaching experience can continue even after the conclusion of our Fulbright award, allowing us to share the mission and vision of the Fulbright program with others throughout our lives.

The future:

Like the physical landscape around this New Hampshire house, the political and professional landscape continues to change. New fields of inquiry have appeared in the wilderness, and new technologies have completely changed research and scholarship in all disciplines.

When the Fulbright program began sixty years ago, there was no gene therapy, no continental drift, no string theory, and no quarks. There were no satellites, no networked computers, and no cell phones. The research tools and protocols in use today are quite different even from those of just ten years ago.

In 40 years, the Fulbright family will be celebrating its centennial. Assuming the Fulbright program still exists, it will still be sending promising young leaders and established experts to the US and other countries to help them achieve their dreams. Even if the program no longer exists, the centennial in 2046 will still be celebrated because thousands and thousands of Fulbright alumni will be alive and active. The young grantees of today, including some who wrote the essays in this collection, will be in their 60s and 70s. Many will still be active in their respective careers, perhaps serving as hosts for visiting scholars themselves.

In forty years from now, education and scholarship will be going in new directions. Our professions will certainly be different, but I submit that the core values and the lessons learned by Fulbright grantees will still be there, influencing their work and their relationships. Regardless of what happens to the Fulbright program, the memories of what happened during an international Fulbright experience will remain, and Fulbright scholars will always be proud members of the "Fulbright family."

Welcome to our house, and I hope you enjoy our stories.

Eric S. Howard
Executive Director
Fulbright Academy of Science & Technology
ehoward@FulbrightAcademy.org

New York
The Big Apple Seen From its Very Core

Alessandra Seggi - Italy

I adore fruit!
It has always been like that, since I was a kid.
For this, in particular, I owe extreme and unconditional gratitude
To my Granny, on my father's side, who,
Proud of her perfect Italian, was always advising me:
"An apple a Day Keeps the Doctor Away!".

Nevertheless,
It was definitely beyond my imagination (and hers too!),
Even though of a very wild, lively, and creative sort,
To think that the discovering and tasting of an a-p-p-l-e,
Even if extraordinary, splendiferous and exceptionally over-sized,
Such as the one in which I live right now,
Could generate such exaltation and joy!

"Your enthusiasm and energy brim over…!"
An American—pretty astonished—exclaims,
While listening to my stories of excitement and wonder.

Yes, I know it,
I am deeply in love with
The Big Apple,
My life
And what I do!

We must not cease from exploring, and the end of all our exploring will be to return from where we came and to know that place for the first time.

~*T.S. Eliot*

First Quarter of the Apple

T-H-E APPLE

Violently: I was impacted with the humidity and the stifling heat of a late August afternoon. I inhaled the penetrating, almost nauseating, smell of the New York City subway system. Upon closing my eyes, I could hear the delirium of the traffic. I opened my eyes again and I filled them with the colors and diversity of the people; their tired eyes, their differing gestures and expressions.

I didn't see the rain until October was almost over. I really thought I was in front of a painting by Seurat; an image created by tapping the top of the paintbrush and dotting the imaginary canvas of my window. Many little raindrops were smudging the buildings; the Riverside Church, the Columbia University Low Library dome, and a little slice of Riverside Park, while peeling bells rendered all this more vivid yet melancholic.

To me, Greenwich Village conveys a whole wagon of tranquility and peace. It is probably because I feel the same atmosphere I felt in The Netherlands, where I lived for an entire year as an undergraduate. It is probably because the streets—those that are narrow and full of details, and those that are a bit wider with slim and tapering sycamores—give me various scents, perfumes, and silences to process and appreciate long after I have experience them. I, then, observe the dark red bricks, the facades of the buildings; clean, neat, one after the other, with black banisters of hammered-iron.

With avidity, I always try to peek through the blinds, inside the windows on the street level. With curiosity, in order to smell something about their worlds, I observe the people going out the main doors. I am looking for stories; I am searching for stories like a hunting dog searches for its prey. I am hunting for stories about vital darkness and light.

And then, yellow, yellow, yellow...as yellow as the stream of cabs running towards me. That yellow color takes me and knocks me down, just like a stormy wave breaking onto the shore, just like the mighty impetus that is about to break down the dam. And then... then, one day, words whispered from the foot of a street lamp catch my attention and I quickly turn towards them: lying on the sidewalk, someone is dragging his life together with a shopping cart and some cardboard boxes.

> And then, Harlem with its loud rhythmic music,
> Chinatown and the convulsing crowd,
> Myths and daily tragedies,
> Dirty walls,
> Garbage on the sidewalk,
> The peace of trees and meadows in Central Park,
> Breathtaking skyscrapers,
> Reflections on mirrors, reflections of mirrors,

Doormen stiff and straight in their uniforms,
Men with their ties and business briefcases,
The No. 7 train, stories of distant planets and long journeys,
Kaleidoscopic tales on stage, on-Broadway and off-Broadway,
Shop windows crammed with goods and some empty life.

Every night, I go back within the four walls of my tiny room, and when the sky seems turned off, the buildings and skyscrapers are turned on. They keep me company and I never feel alone.

Second Quarter of the Apple

INTERNATIONAL HOUSE

They say it is a "dorm for graduate students", but I believe it must be some sort of typo. Created in 1920, thanks to the philanthropy of John D. Rockefeller Jr., it looks like Wonderland. Situated in front of Riverside Church, close to Riverside Park; International House is home to over seven hundred graduate students in New York. They come from more countries than I am able to spot on an atlas, speak more languages than I could ever list, and pursue any kind of study possible and imaginable…

A genuine sense of community can be seen within the President of International House, Donald Cuneo: an open and generous smile, a wide forehead, eyes that continuously dance from right to left in order to embrace more and more people, and a remote tie to "my" Italy, revealed through his last name…

International House is an extraordinary self-governing microcosm teeming with life and activity: bazaars and convenience stores, together with the study center, a small library, and a cozy dining room. Then, there are washing machines, a copy machine, fax machine, gym, basketball court, computer lab, fitness center, a coffee house and even a bar!

Alessandra Seggi – Italy

The frontispiece on the building's main façade reads "That Brotherhood May Prevail." And each International House resident does his or her best to put this principle into practice, every day. In fact, at International House, social life fosters communication, cultural exchange, and understanding. In our main lounge, in the extraordinarily wide and welcoming Davis Hall, in the Mural Room that reminds me of old days with my granny, and in the Dodge Room (warm and hospitable thanks to dark wood pieces of furniture), we have innumerable activities to please everyone. We have roundtables, although without King Arthur and his brave knights, panel discussions, language exchange hours (virtually any language!), cooking sessions, cultural hours, the Fall Fiesta,[1] ballroom dancing (to burn the calories accumulated during and after the above-mentioned cooking sessions!) and more and much more.

The majority of these activities take place thanks to the volunteering of residents. I have been involved in the International House Tutorial Program and, every week, I have been spending time with an adorable six-year-old kid with black and curly hair. She does her homework with me, draws funny faces (that turn out to be my portraits) or together, we read fairy tales. I hope I have been able to provide her with some spontaneity, enthusiasm, and positive stimuli. In exchange, I have been receiving lots of smiles, huge hugs, and lots of love.

In addition to this, I was selected to join the Women's International Leadership (WIL) Program; probably one of the most successful and rich programs at International House. Throughout the weekend seminars and workshops take place. The one-year WIL Program is designed to hone and develop the "fifteen distinguished participants" international understanding and leadership skills. Needless to say, it has been a fruitful and challenging experience for me.

---

[1] Thanks to this gorgeous parade of the traditional costumes from every country, I was ashamed to discover I did not know what *my* national costume was!

At this point, if you are comfortable with the fact that International House is just like Wonderland, you won't find it too hard to stretch it a bit more and see me as the White Hare (my totally white, plain yogurt, fair complexion suits the role perfectly!) or the Mad Hatter… In fact, since I am always trying to throw birthday parties that nobody is willing to attend (due to their super-demanding, hyper-intense academic programs), I am as c-r-r-r-azy as the Mad Hatter, and always running off somewhere in haste, always trying to be in two different places at the same time, always in a perpetual hurry, greeting people in a mixture of ItaliSpanEnglish, always trying to go against any reasonable and solidly proven laws of Time and Physics and to catch the 8:30 a.m. bus even though it's already 8:45 a.m.; I am just like the White Hare! The only difference between the White Hare and me, if you will, is that, unfortunately, I do not possess that gorgeous, flashy, silver pocket watch that he received and showed off, from Mister Lewis C.'s bounty.

Third Quarter of the Apple

THE NEW SCHOOL

When I got to the Big Apple, I was very concerned about my academic performance, since I had never been to the U.S. let alone studied at an American university. I was worried I would not be able to integrate or to adjust myself to this new and mysterious U.S. academic system. I was also worried about the different approach, the different evaluation system, and the strong academic competition here…

And, at the beginning, I used to wake up at 3 o'clock in the morning (I must confess that time zones played a key role in this: 3:00 a.m. in New York corresponds to 9:00 a.m. in Italy!). Well, I used to wake up at 3 o'clock in the morning having nightmares about my being kicked out of school and sent straight back home, due to highly unsatisfactory academic performance! Thank God, things went differently, in fact very differently.

The first class I took, Foundations of Media Theory, gave me the possibility to brush up on Plato and the myth of the cave! What emotion! What an exhilarating experience! I had abandoned Plato together with dusty memories of tenth grade and the curves of supply and demand from my business studies. It was like plunging myself into the peaceful sea of my past life and becoming able to link all the knowledge I had gained until then into an extraordinary new and richer reality. And, needless to say, I am still extremely happy that I did so. Really, to me, it has never mattered how demanding my instructors have been and how close the deadlines for my various assignments and papers have been. I have always been going from one study center to another, from one library to another, proud, excited, and eager to know all the secrets about Media Studies.

In my beloved Italy, I used to attend university lectures in huge classrooms (with an average of 500/600 students), where the professor –nothing but a tiny little black living speck, miles away from me—was always running frantically from one side to the other of a never-ending whiteboard, scribbling figures and curves unreadable to my poor short-sighted eyes. For this reason, I think it is extraordinary to gather around a table with my Understanding Cybernetics' professor, together with ten other students or so. In fact, I do like and appreciate the informality of this academic protocol (that—being informal—is a protocol by no means!). I appreciate the faculty members' availability and openness. Besides, I like the interdisciplinary approach, the emphasis on your own ideas and self-expression. And I am thrilled by the possibility of following my inclinations and developing my interests in every class. Besides here I am asked to write essays that reflect my interiorizing and elaborating on the information I absorb. Back home, during painful in-class written and oral exams, I was questioned about my knowledge of facts and figures rather than being asked to demonstrate my critical and analytical abilities.

Here I have access to many libraries throughout the city, and I have the opportunity to attend several free seminars and workshops organized by the university. Then, last December, when I heard that the computer lab remained open 24 hours a day, my jaw dropped and I remained speechless for quite a while (well, maybe for less than 24 hours, though, as some of my dear friends have remarked, underscoring my irresistibly talkative nature). Once again, back home, I was used to a more restricted and limited availability of high tech instruments and machinery.

In addition to this, in Italy, I was left to my own academic destiny: I used to live and perform my academic activities without any real official faculty representative or contact person's support. At The New School, I have a Student Advisor, a Student Coordinator at the Department of Film and Media Studies, and another Advisor at the International Student Office. Then, I have one more Advisor at the Institute of International Education (IIE) and an entire staff at my disposal at the Fulbright Commission, in Rome, Italy! Not to mention the free tickets to concerts, musicals, and ballet that "the wonderful team"—consisting of Stephanie, Don, and Inge—offers on a weekly basis, at the IIE Events Desk! Well, do you believe me when I say that I do not feel lonely and abandoned to my obscure academic destiny any more?

Fourth Quarter of the Apple

LIFE BETWEEN THE NEW AND OLD WORLD

I take risks and I force the people I love to take risks too, despite their unwillingness to do so. I multiply the uncertainties of my life every single moment. I fuel my life with the challenging and the unknown, rather than the familiar and the old. I truly live on smells, scents, colors, spaces, lights, people, always new and different. And every time I go back to the usual, every time I see again a familiar light, something breaks down inside of me: I lose my old *un*stable balance and I acquire a new, delicate, *un*stable one. Every time I go back and then I leave again, every time I abandon my roots, my domestic roots, my hills' roots, my father and mother's roots, something is torn again. Inside of me and inside all those who love me, something is torn, just like a piece of fabric in the hands of some nervous or expert tailor.

My life is made of tears, of quick intercontinental calls, too short to impress you, but still long enough to leave you uneasy and puzzled. My life is made of lacerations, of eyes that want to cry, of sad moods, never really expressed and released, of misty and gloomy looks, of eyes downcast. My life is full of mementos; it's full of stories, memories, and pictures hard to store since I am always moving around. My life is made of timid and courageous steps on a rope between two trees: the Old and the New World.

Nevertheless, I profoundly want this experience. I need these odors, these scents, lights, spaces, colors, always new and different. I want to enjoy these new faces; I want to appreciate this American English, its rhythm and its meanings, its various forms and sounds. I want to explore the people I meet, understand life, taste and appreciate it in all its dimensions, with the care of the craftsman, with the wit of the artist. I want to devour this Master's that opened up new details and unimaginable nuances for me.

And when I am in this frame of mind, I forget about the lacerations of my life in between two worlds. I forget the blindness of those who live only on certainty and routine and do not comprehend my choice of being in America. I forget about the ties that went broken or will come loose with many people back home. I forget about my inability to share daily news and chats after lunch with many dear people who remain in the Old World. I forget that, perhaps, back home, someone was forced to do without me.

And I forget the fatigue, nights spent reading books, studying in a library, or typing in front of a computer. I forget that I need to sleep sometimes and I cannot do everything I would like to do. I forget I often give up the sun in order to enjoy the bright light shining from a renowned professor or from one of my favorite instructors.

And when I think that I have had the chance to observe both the light and dark sides of life, worlds of enthusiasm and desperation, I cannot help but continuing the fight. My contribution to this world is through my daily life, lived intensely, to the best of my abilities, through my strong determination to enjoy the sun even when I can't see it, and through my ability to share this delicious A-p-p-l-e with all who feel like listening to me…

Before and After the Apple

Before the Apple there I was: a 28 year-old graduate in Business and Economics from the University of Genoa, Italy. At the time, my existence was filled with life as an analyst in an insurance company in Milan. I spent my work days dissecting balance sheets, entertaining my colleagues with impressions of cartoon voices, and guessing the various authors of the verses that my big boss amused us by reciting. I was in fact the clown of the office. Everybody seemed to like me… Never did it cross their minds to let me go; and, honestly, there was no reason for me to leave them either. Nevertheless, I did.

I left them all, dear colleagues and charming bosses, after I received a phone call, a very special one, on a summer day. "May I speak with Alessandra Seggi, please?" uttered an American-accented female voice inside the handset I was so unsurely holding in my right hand. "Speaking," I answered tentatively, sensing and hoping for something great to happen, but cautiously fearing the worst. "This is the Fulbright Commission in Rome, *Dottoressa* Seggi. You have been awarded the scholarship! The New School in New York has accepted your application," the voice close to my right ear continued calmly. And that voice tried in vain to soothe the confusion that was just then exploding in my head. "Can you talk right now, *Dottoressa* Seggi?" the voice on the phone was quick to add, anticipating my discomfort. "Gosh," I mumbled to myself, swallowing deeply. "Oh, my gosh," I repeated in disbelief and I answered back: "No, I can't."

That phone call was the beginning of the longest and most intense weekend in my life. I was in fact left with a huge decision to make: leave or stay? Accept the scholarship and for the first time cross the Atlantic Ocean, or stay and keep amusing my colleagues daily, in Milan? Start studying again in New York City, capital of the world, or keep my job, which was flourishing and giving me financial independence? Risk a little and go, or keep working in Milan and commute, every weekend, to Sant'Olcese, the village where I grew up and my parents lived? Dare to really stretch myself and make new multicultural friends in America or fulfill my parents' expectations for a life made of a routine 9-to-5 job, a husband, some kids, and Sundays with parents and in-laws?

Leave or stay? Leave? Or stay? That weekend, while I was consumed by the dilemma, Sant'Olcese, with its 5,000 inhabitants scattered in un-picturesque hamlets on hills filled with olive and cherry trees, seemed so beautiful and hospitable. I felt almost smitten by its peace, and jealous of its stark immobility and cozy warmth. I had not gone anywhere yet, and yet I was already missing it all. On the other hand, while torn in that dichotomy trying to make the "right" decision, I had the sense that, somehow, I was forgetting to take into consideration other characteristics of my village. Was I forgetting the many lacks—of dreams, of initiative, of imagination, of ambition, and of courage—in my fellow villagers? Was I forgetting the superficiality and pettiness of gossipy conversations at the hairdresser's or the baker's? Was I forgetting the subtle bigotry of some church-goers, the provinciality of those who did not encourage me to leave, the perhaps unspoken jealousy of friends, relatives, and acquaintances? And finally, was I forgetting the astonishing narrow-mindedness of those who, ensconced in their safe routine, apparently opposed my scholarship and what it entailed? Or, on the contrary, was I giving these factors too much weight? So I went back and forth, sometimes favoring one side, sometimes the other. Tough decision-making really swings back and forth like this, I guess.

To make my life more miserable, there was even an unexpected and suddenly strong desire to have a child. "How could I possibly have a child if I go to America and dedicate myself to studying again?" I was saying to myself, panicking. My brain was fast to picture dark scenarios and draw hasty conclusions: how could I raise a child anyway, without the love of their grandparents on their mother's side? How could I have a child in the first place, if I'm single and getting old, fast and furiously?

And then there was the thought of my mother tormenting me and making my decision-making process even more painful: my mother, the person whom I adored most completely and unconditionally in the world. There she was, simple and wise, to make my life unwittingly even harder. I could not stop thinking about how much she had suffered, how much she had lost in her life (her father, when she was barely a year old, and her mother, when she was almost twelve). I was focused on how many humiliations she had told me she had undergone in her early life; how much she had done for me; and how much she loved me. How could I possibly do "this" to her? How could I dare to "leave" her? How could I "leave" her and start afresh in the New World without her?

My worries really seemed to be churned out relentlessly, with no respite in sight. Last but not least, there were my feelings: a delicate and explosive mixture of hellish fear, excitement, resignation, pride, worry, anticipation, anxiety, deep sorrow, and utter confusion. At the time I did not have any idea that these feelings were, in fact, influencing and being influenced by all those clashing elements. I am referring to all the factors I was examining in my head: my pride in being financially independent, my eagerness to explore the world, my fellow villagers' perceived shortcomings, my desire for a child, and my worry about my mother. Only much later in my life did I come to understand how that dynamic process of mutual shaping happens: our inner and social lives are dramatically connected through an osmotic process that allows them to communicate and exchange vital elements. That realization has been both freeing and constraining. On the one hand, it is finally clear to me I cannot attribute my inner workings solely to my free will; there is something in the outside world affecting my most personal decisions. On the other, it is constraining in the sense that it is very difficult to understand exactly how it all plays itself out.

Unexpectedly, though, while I was fighting to make my decision, my parents, and my mother in particular, offered me genuine support in addition to what I thought was selfless advice. "If you go," my mother uttered out of the blue, "of course, it will be *you* who will have to study and work hard. But," she added fast, "it seems to us [to herself and my father] that this scholarship is a great opportunity." That observation came like a security blanket for me: it made me feel safer and less alone while I was considering whether to accept the scholarship or not; it made me feel that my parents were on my side, rooting for me, wanting what *I* wanted. If I decided to go, my parents even promised to chip in if I needed some money. And only God knows how easy it is to need money in New York City! Besides, what made their promise special was the fact that my parents are not rich people, not big magnates, not high-scale business people but very good-hearted, always meaning well, and strong-willed. Since time immemorial, they have been breaking their backs in Sant'Olcese, running a tiny hardware store and, before some oil company's restructuring forced them to give it up, a gas station too. Long hours, very few, if any, diversions, and many sacrifices characterize my parents' frugal existence. In their unsophisticated world view, they had nevertheless seemed to sense what was important to the development of a young mind. And they had always offered money for the exciting human unfolding of their only child.

In fact, in high school, it was with my parents' money that I had gone to Great Britain to improve my English; I treasured every minute of that rainy two-week trip. After high school, it was with my parents' money that I had gone to college, when no one else in the family had done it. I had gone to college but had unfortunately "chosen" (pushed by my parents and advised by my high school English teacher) the convenient track for making money and getting a job—Business and Economics—instead of following a path more congenial to my natural gifts—Languages. While in college, again, it was with a European Union Scholarship and some of my parents' money that I had been able to study in The Netherlands for a year, learning how to make business plans and getting a vivid sense of what it means to communicate beyond barriers.

But now, after the Apple, after having savored three years of the Fulbright experience, I believe there had been strings attached to that money and support that my parents had so generously offered. "When are you coming back for good?" was the annoying expression I heard each time I spoke with them on the phone while I was still in America. That expression was the tip of the iceberg of a whole unspoken illusion my parents had entertained: they had never really wanted me to leave; they had wanted me home. Close to them. Within their reach. Filling their emptiness with my physical presence. "Why didn't they just tell me?" and "Why didn't they voice their sorrow?" I ask myself, astonished. Childless, I am unable to comprehend the laws and secrets of parenthood. I have given these questions quite some thought since I completed my program. Simple and straightforward answers are hard to come by and even harder to accept. Nevertheless, I wish my parents had been more open and more aware of what I perceive as their need for me in their lives. I wish I had not found myself entangled in that sticky web of emotionally charged statements. I wish I had been more free to live.

But life is never too easy and straightforward, right? Over time, things have gotten somewhat worse. Now that, after my Fulbright experience and my Master's, I have chosen to extend my stay in America and pursue a Ph.D., I am sure my mother regrets having encouraged me to accept that scholarship. Now, after six years "without me," that "when-are-you-coming-back" refrain has gotten more oppressive and more ominous. "When are you planning to get real and settle down?" is the new slogan uttered with no discernable embarrassment not only by my parents but even by family and friends.

What should I do? Should I drop everything and go back to Italy? Mom, Dad; I am speaking to you now: I am truly sorry I am so impractical and my dreams are so big and unconventional. I am also sorry I'm not interested in a 9 to 5 job close to your village. I am sorry I want to dig deep inside myself, uncover my self, and let myself grow. I am sorry I like ideas more than possessions. I am sorry I'm apparently careless about my "pensione" [retirement plan] and money. I am sorry you seem to be suffering when I am not home with you. I am sorry your plans and hopes for me do not coincide with my own. I am sorry if you think I let you down. And I am sorry you are struggling with the idea that I am a grown-up woman and that I have a life of my own. But one thing I am not sorry about: I want to live my life fully and responsibly.

A Final Note for the Prospective Fulbright Scholar

Let yourself go. Dream big. Stretch your wings. Fly. Let your whole being take in your Fulbright experience. Let it really sink in. And when it's time for you to go back to your country of origin and give back to your community, you will find yourself a transformed person: deeper, richer, wiser, and more complex.

P.S. To be perfectly honest with myself and my readers, I want to disclose a last piece of information. Now that I am just about to put my pen down, doubts are rising in my head again: have I managed to give a reasonably objective description of what happened? Have I been true to myself and the people I described? Have I been biased? Perhaps are the destructive voices from Sant'Olcese reclaiming me? My journey is not finished yet, I guess.

aleseggi@fulbrightweb.org

From Makerere to Stanford: The Experience of a Fulbright Scholar

Winnie Tarinyeba - Uganda

Wednesday 20th April 2005 will forever be engrained in my mind. An otherwise ordinary day turned out to be the day I became a scholar. It had been a long and tiring day and I was scheduled to teach a late evening class from 7-9 PM. The internet connection at the Law School was down so I went to an internet café in the City for a routine ten minute email session. I expected nothing more than emails from friends and a few spam. I was totally unprepared for what I found. There were four emails from Krista Andersen, the Administrative Director of the International Graduate Programs at Stanford Law School informing me that they were holding a place for me as a Fulbright scholar for the academic year 2005/6 at Stanford Law School. It was one of the greatest moments of my life: the prayers, the long wait, the trouble of taking GRE examinations, the interviews, the long application process and the opportunity of a long sought after career path had finally come true. It all seemed like a dream, but unlike fiction, the dream was real and the good Lord had let his light shine upon me once again. Twenty four years ago when my father was murdered by Government agents, my mother was not sure she would see us through elementary school and now an offer to study at one of the finest Universities in the world was right in front of me - it was more than a miracle.

I was among the five lucky Fulbright grantees from Uganda for the 2005-2006 academic year that had been selected after a long and competitive application process that had begun in July 2004. At the orientation in Uganda, before we departed, it was very clear that the five of us were indeed very lucky. We shared experiences about the application process, and the anxiety and hopes for a fulfilling career path. As we sat through the orientation conducted by officials of the American Embassy in Uganda[2], it was all broad smiles. At the orientation, we were given literature about the US, about being a foreign student in the US, the US map and Fulbright badges. I wore my badge with great pride and gratitude. I was now a Fulbright scholar and could identify with Fulbright scholars serving in various capacities all over the world and making a contribution to the betterment of society.

I left Uganda on 8th August 2005 for a very long journey to Stanford. It took me 24 hours including the stopovers to arrive at my final destination. Under normal circumstances, such a journey should be exhausting with severe jet lag. However, I was as strong, excited, energetic and high spirited when I arrived at Stanford as I was when I left home. The beautiful and extensive campus was breath taking. As we entered the campus through Palm Drive, I could not help but notice the beauty of the surroundings and marvel at this opportunity of a lifetime. I arrived alone at San Jose International Airport and although it was my first time in the United States, I was confident that I would find my way. My first encounter with the kindness of the American people in the United States was with the taxi driver who drove me from the airport to the university. He was very kind

---

[2] Catherine Kiwanuka and Dorothy Ngalombi of the Public Affairs office at the American Embassy in Uganda were very supportive.

and told me about the towns we drove through, including San Jose and Palo Alto. He told me what he knew about Stanford and when we got to the university he not only helped me locate the student housing office, but also helped me find a place to buy something to eat and helped me carry my luggage to a place that was to be home for the next year.

I was allocated housing in a three bedroom apartment on campus and when I moved in, I found a student who had spent six years at Stanford, both as an undergraduate and graduate student. Kelsey Lynn was completing her Masters Degree in Mechanical Engineering. We only lived together for two weeks before she moved out to another house on campus that had been allocated to her. However, in two weeks Kelsey and I had become very good friends. She is one of the amazing people I have met in my life and certainly the first female rugby player I have met. She helped me settle in and was very eager to learn about my country. I have learnt so much about the US from her. I also found that Kelsey and I shared the same faith and she was very kind to offer me a ride to church every Sunday. She introduced me to her mother and several friends. We agreed to have lunch once every week and on Sundays. Studying abroad can be a challenging and very lonely experience; however, with a friend like Kelsey I was less nostalgic. Her kindness changed my perception about Americans and challenged my own attitude towards people. It is not uncommon to find that many times we are blinded by our own prejudices about people and as a result we not only unfairly judge others, but miss out on opportunities for meaningful relationships. I have made several other friends including Marketa Trimble from the Czeck Republic, Tierno Balde from Guinea, Annie Wilkinson, Hannah, Leila, Anneeleen Steeno, all whom have in different ways enriched my understanding about their own cultures and countries.

There has been so much to experience and to see in the US. My first adventure was to tour San Francisco. We explored the city on our bikes, and my favorite part was the famous Golden Gate Bridge. The love parade in San Francisco and (in my opinion, crazy) Halloween parties were all very exciting. The Fulbright contact office in San Francisco arranged for me and another Fulbright student, Pedro Alives to spend thanksgiving with a host family in Palo Alto-Gordon and Sandra Short and their three very lovely children Felicity, Andres and Mayerly. I attended a thanksgiving ceremony with the family at their local church and thereafter went home for the traditional thanksgiving meal-turkey and pumpkin pie. Pedro and I were very thrilled to learn about the history of this special US holiday. I feel very privileged to have experienced a part of the American culture.

I have often been asked whether I experienced a culture shock when I arrived in the US and to my surprise I did not. The US is the world's greatest nation and a land of opportunity in every sense of the word. However, to my surprise, I have not only met some very nice people, but found that in the US, they too struggle with most of the issues that we struggle with in other parts of the world, including poverty, unemployment, access to health care and crime. The one thing that surprised me, however, was that many Americans are deeply religious. This was contrary to my perceptions about the American society and what is projected about one of the United States' most fundamental constitutional principals - the separation of church and state; as well as assumptions that in highly industrialized countries, people become self-sufficient and disregard religion[3]. There is a notion that technological and scientific advances as well as increase in wealth and well-being drive people away from God because of the security that they provide. This is not entirely true for America. The reverse is certainly true in poor countries where people struggle for the most basic needs through out their entire life, with high infant mortality rates and low life expectancy. God, religion and other sacred beliefs still play an important role in people's lives.

---

[3] I once asked a church minister at Cambridge why the English who were very instrumental in spreading Christianity had abandoned religion and he said when people become self sufficient, there is a tendency to think they do not need God.

As a lawyer, I was also curious to learn about the American society that is often publicized as litigious. As I pushed my trolley at the airport, I accidentally knocked a lady and she said to me "I will sue you". I said to me, "yes this is America" and quickly apologized. I had watched various movies where the police informed arrested persons of their rights - the Miranda warning (a practice that is not common in other jurisdictions) and was happy to learn about the practice. It arose out of a Supreme Court case Miranda vs. Arizona[4] where convictions of robbery, kidnapping and rape against Ernesto Miranda were overturned because the court found that during interrogation by the police he had been intimidated and had not understood his right not to incriminate himself. The court ruled that a person in custody must, prior to interrogation, be clearly informed that he has the right to remain silent, and that anything he says will be used against him in court; he must be clearly informed that he has the right to consult with an attorney and to have that attorney present during interrogation, and that, if he is indigent, an attorney will be provided at no cost to represent him. On a rather cynical note, we were informed by one of our professors that Miranda became a victim of his own warning. He was stabbed and as he lay down before he died, he heard the police give his assailant the Miranda warning. I had also heard about the ridiculous law suits and huge awards granted by juries such as the lady who had washed her cat and put it in the micro wave to dry and sued the micro wave company when it died, the lady who bought hot coffee from McDonalds, put it between her thighs as she drove then got burnt when it spilled and sued McDonalds, the burglar who fell as he attempted to break into a house and sued the owner of the house. As it turned out, most of the stories were either not true or often misrepresented by the media. What I learned was that most people in the US are aware about their rights and therefore claim conscious. The legal system encourages access to courts and makes it easy and cheap to file claims[5]. Class action suits and the fact that each party bears its own costs of litigation, make courts

---

[4] 384 US 436 (1966).
[5] It costs about 120 dollars to file a suit in the US.

more accessible hence the notion that Americans are litigious. This is only part of the picture. While, it is easy to file a suit in the US, many suits never go to trial. Most suits either get settled or the parties lose interest and abandon them. This is because of a process that is unique to the US legal system: the discovery process. This allows parties to obtain as much information form each other prior to the trial. The majority of suits get settled as a result of this process.

I was admitted to the Stanford Program in International Legal Studies (SPILS) at the Stanford Law School. Stanford University is currently ranked as the third best university in the world[6] and the Law School is also ranked 3rd in the US[7]. I feel very privileged to be a part of this great institution. We are 13 students on the SPILS program. It is primarily designed for international scholars and this year the countries represented on the program are as Israel(3), the Czech Republic, Germany, Guinea, Japan, Taiwan, Romania, Turkey, Switzerland, Mexico and myself from Uganda. The diversity amongst us contributes to the richness of the program. We all bring our country experiences and perceptions to the discussions. The program is very competitive and to have been selected from the 80 or more applicants is quite a blessing.

Having studied in the United Kingdom before, I did not experience a culture shock when I came to the United States. The quality of life and facilities available are far beyond the imagination of a Ugandan student. The library facilities, teaching aides, computer and online resource facilities are amazing. On many occasions I would stop to think about the resource challenges at Makerere University. The Faculty of Law at Makerere, where I was once a student, has a computer lab with about eight computers serving a student population of about 1200. It is no surprise that somebody can graduate without ever having used a computer. The University has only one library,

---

[6] http://ed.sjtu.cn/rank
[7] J. Paul Lomio & Erika V. Wayne, Ranking of Top Law Schools 1987-2006. http://juris.stanford.edu/library/RANK20052006.pdf

which was built in 1963 and continues to serve the ever growing student population. Stanford on the other hand has 21 libraries, all sufficiently stocked with hard copy and electronic resources. I have learnt that Stanford Law School collaborates with law schools in Latin America, and I intend to explore the possibility of collaboration with the Law School at Makerere University. The one thing that took me by surprise was the professors. They take time to know the students and their interests. The degree of interest and effort made to do this surprised me. Not only are they always willing to help, but to my astonishment I found that all the Professors I needed to work with had background information about me and knew my research interests. This was not only a pleasant surprise but a challenge to me as a young Assistant Lecturer at Makerere University back home. The Socratic method of teaching is another unique feature about the American system. Every Professor made it clear in the first week of class that class participation was important. This was very different from the traditional method of instruction that most of us were used to-where the professor lectures to the students and apart from the few hardworking and interested students in class, the rest participate passively. The advantages of the Socratic method of teaching are rather obvious- the classroom discussions and free atmosphere of exchanging views and ideas enriches the learning experience and is a great tool for building character and confidence.

I must however, mention that graduate study in the United States is a daunting experience, especially for foreign students. I recall in the first week we were all overwhelmed by the assignments and the amount of work we had to do to prepare for classes. Questions such as whether we were expected to read all the materials that professors assigned for each class were not uncommon. I was particularly shocked in one class when the professor assigned us a book to read and said we were to discuss it within a week's time. This was one out of five courses I was taking, and all required sufficient preparation before class in addition to the weekly assignments; it seemed impossible. The good news is I eventually adapted and now even enjoy the work.

I was also amazed by the level of analysis. The courses are not designed to simply teach legal rules, but to offer opportunity for analytical thinking about the rationale and efficiency of the rules. I found heavy emphasis on economic efficiency of legal rules and legal reasoning. The interdisciplinary approach to legal scholarship was not only interesting, but a practical approach to academic training in this day and age. Much to my surprise, I was advised by one of my professors to take a course in economics. The interdisciplinary training I have received is perhaps the most valuable training I have received so far. The importance attached to interdisciplinary research and the huge research agenda in the US has opened my eyes to a wide range of things. I now fully appreciate the importance of research and academic debate. In one of my courses[8] we were exposed to academic debate among various US scholars on the issue of law and social norms. It was interesting to see how academic scholars respond to another. The issue in this particular case was about the power of norms as tools for regulating social control[9]. The exposure to the US legal system will be particularly helpful for comparative studies.

There are three other things that I have found very unique to the American system: networking, career guidance and interaction with professors. As foreign students, most of us were shocked when we were introduced to the concept of networking. This involves establishing contacts with potential employers for purposes of getting jobs and future interaction. At the schools, seminars on how to network and the importance of networking were conducted. We

---

[8] Interdisciplinary Legal Scholarship by Jonathan Greenberg.
[9] See R.H Coase, *The Problem of Social Cost* 3J.L &Econ.1(1960), C. Ellickson, Order Without Law: How Neighbors Settle Disputes. Cambridge, Mass., Harvard University Press (1991), Eric Posner, Law and Social Norms. Cambridge, Mass., Harvard University Press (2000), Lawrence Lessig, *The New Chicago School.* 27 J. LEGAL STUD 661 (1998) and

found this rather bizarre but nevertheless an interesting concept. The law school also has a fully fledged office of career services. They coordinate on-campus interviews, offer training on drafting resumes and cover letter and conduct mock interviews as well as provide advice on job searching. I have not previously attended an institution with such services and I found their services valuable.

The law school has a deliberate policy to encourage interaction between professors and students. Every student has an opportunity to take a professor to lunch and have the expenses reimbursed by the Law School. In addition, the law school and student organizations organize various events intended to encourage students and professors to interact and share experiences. One example is the meetings with the Stanford Women Law Panel where the female members of the faculty share their experiences with students. At the International Law Panel, the professors shared their experiences about their research and work at various international forums.

The scholarship I was awarded was a Fulbright Junior Staff Development Grant, designed to give opportunities to junior professionals in academic institutions to advance their careers. I have already mentioned that I am an Assistant Lecturer at the Faculty of Law Makerere University. I was appointed initially as a Teaching Assistant and was subsequently promoted to Assistant Lecturer after attaining a Master of Laws Degree from the University of Cambridge in the United Kingdom[10]. The terms of my appointment included, among others that I should register for a PhD within in two years. This was the natural course of action if I wanted to get full tenure as a Professor. The rule is not strictly enforced because the University is not in a position to provide adequate funding for the staff to pursue further studies. However, one cannot progress in their academic career without a PhD. Therefore, it was crucial for me to look for

---

[10] Robert Weisberg, *Norms and Criminal Law and the Norms of Criminal Law Scholarship* 93 J. Crim. L & Criminology 467 (2002-2003)

funding. I applied to some Universities and although I was admitted everywhere, financial assistance, continued to be an obstacle. Because this had been my dream since I was an undergraduate student at the very institution that I was now teaching at, I was very frustrated by the financial barrier. During my undergraduate years, I was particularly inspired by one of my professors, who is currently the Deputy Vice Chancellor in charge of Academic Affairs at Makerere University, Dr. Lillian Tibatemwa-Ekirikubinza. She taught me Criminal Law and was very impressive in class. She is one of my mentors and it was very gratifying to work with her as a colleague and friend at the faculty of law. The other person who has greatly inspired me is Dr. Eilis Ferran, a Professor at Cambridge. She taught me Corporate Finance and was one of my referees for my application for the Fulbright scholarship. When I wrote to inform her I had been awarded the scholarship and was going to Stanford, she wrote, "Winnie, this is brilliant news. Warmest congratulations. Please keep in touch. I'm very interested in following your stellar career!"

I have very fond memories of the beginning of my career. I started work in September 2001. I was aware that life as an academic scholar can be very demanding and challenging, especially in a poor country such as Uganda. However, for me it was a dream come true and I was prepared to do everything possible to walk in the footsteps of my mentors. The most challenging aspect was finding funding for further studies. On many occasions, this seemed an uphill task. My hopes were renewed when the American Embassy in Uganda wrote to the Dean informing him that there were opportunities for the Fulbright Junior Staff Development Scholarships. The Dean informed us about it and for me that was the beginning of a long process that eventually got me to Stanford Law School.

The grant from Fulbright covered my tuition, living expenses, settling in allowance, books and computer allowance, roundtrip air ticket as well as accident and health insurance. I also received a supplemental award from the Delta Kappa Gamma Society International. It is a generous grant and because of it I have been able to concentrate on my studies without being distracted by financial worries. The events and programs organized by Fulbright such as the tours, benefit dinners, subsidized group opera shows and professional enrichment programs have enabled me to meet other Fulbright scholars, to learn about the American culture and the people who generously contribute to the program. The experience is both enlightening and enriching.

The time that I have spent in the US has also enabled me to be an ambassador for my country. I have learnt about other cultures and also helped others learn about my own country and its culture. It was very interesting to learn that people hardly knew about my country. Unfortunately many who had heard about Uganda knew the negative aspects such as the HIV/AIDS scourge or the dictatorial regimes of Iddi Amin and Milton Obote (both of whom are deceased now). At times, I was asked about the level of development in Uganda amidst many other questions. Fortunately for me, I arrived in the US shortly after the G8 summit in Gleneagles, Scotland where the summit had agreed to cancel the debt of the 18 poorest countries in the World, which included Uganda. That proved to be a convenient starting point. I have held discussions with several people on various issues about Uganda including politics, women emancipation, education, HIV/AIDS, war and several others. I have made presentations to gatherings outside the university about Uganda including the University Rotary Club of Palo Alto and members of a local church. I am glad that I had the opportunity to share experiences with these people about Uganda. My stay in the US has not only enabled me to advance my career, but to broaden my understanding of other cultures and connect with diverse people. Kelsey plans to visit Uganda: this for me is confirmation of the value of cultural exchange as envisioned by Senator J. William Fulbright when he started this program. His vision has brought many to the US and given opportunity to millions of students including myself to pursue our dream careers. I am grateful for the opportunity and I hope that I, too, will give back to society in the same measure.

wtarinye@stanford.edu

Five Definitions of America (My Fulbright Journey)

Zeeshan-ul-hassan Usmani
- Pakistan

The Journey Starts:

My hometown, Sukkur, is located next to the Indus River in the province of Sind, Pakistan. It is a comparatively small town with no two-lane roads, university or public transportation. The best way to commute within the city is still by horse-carriages and in addition, donkeys are used to carry stuff. The temperature climbs as high as 55 degrees Celsius (131 degrees Fahrenheit) in the summer and the local language is Sindhi. Why am I telling you all this? So that you can understand the effect and extent the cultural shock experienced by me compared to the cultural shock experienced by a person coming from big cities like Karachi, Lahore, or Islamabad.

After my graduation, I started looking for possible scholarships and admission opportunities in developed countries. There were so many countries on the list - China, Japan, Cyprus, Australia, Germany, Italy, France, Switzerland, Canada, UK and USA. After careful consideration and visiting various websites of universities, inquiring about their research facilities, finding their positions on international rankings and speaking with so many foreign graduates, the US started to become the only wise choice. The next question was: Affordability. Coming from a humble background it seemed impossible without having a jackpot! Then, there was another list of scholarship agencies, ranging from the British Council to the Commonwealth Scholarship, the Higher Education Commission (HEC) of Pakistan to the Bill Gates Fund. Fulbright was not on the list until I saw an advertisement in a daily newspaper. I applied for it and then there came the day that changed my life, my mind, my goals, my objective and my way of thinking; September 19, 2003. I got an email from the US Education Foundation in Pakistan to appear for my Fulbright scholarship interview on September 22nd 2003 at 5:30 P.M in the Islamabad office.

My interview went quite well except for my comments regarding the USA. I had a very wrong impression about the USA and its people. In response to one of the questions, I replied: the USA loves to go to war; either it is Afghanistan or Iraq. My interviewer even asked me "Do you hate the USA?" and I said "No." But I thought to myself that I did not have any reason to love it.

When, in July 2003, I went for my visa interview at the US Embassy in Islamabad, it was incredibly hot; people outside Pakistan cannot imagine the heat of July. There I was, standing with some 200 people in the line outside the US embassy waiting for my turn to be called for an interview. There was no cooling system, no fan, or even water. The US seems to spend all its money on wars, yet does not have a few hundred rupees to put a fan here, I thought! When somebody called my name: "OozMani," I was sure that it was my turn.

I was given the VISA and the scholarship. I was so happy, thrilled, and excited; all living and non-living objects I had a chance to talk with on my way to the USA know now that I received a Fulbright scholarship. In September 2004 (not 2001), I reached America – **"The Land of Prejudice"** (according to my earlier definition).

To get accustomed with the United States and its culture, I read every single travelogue available in my city at that time, and it did not change my definition of America to **"The Land of Prejudice, Nudity and Drunken People."** So there I was, with my most recent researched view of America.

Welcome to America - My First Day:

The first person I met at Newark International airport was a black woman. Lucas was her name. She took me to her office for routine questions, and the first question she asked was "What is your name?"

"Zeeshan-ul-hassan Usmani" – I replied.

"Speak in English," she said.

Oh my God! I can not translate my name into English, and it is so embarrassing when you are speaking in English with someone and he or she cannot understand you!

Anyway, after a brief and nice Q&A session I got out of the airport, and either of the two things I was expecting had not happened. First, (as portrayed by our media after 9/11) the unbelievable security checking usually involves an officer 'requesting' you to remove your articles of clothing one by one, and the second (as documented by our famous travelogue writers) is a group of beautiful girls welcoming you as soon as you enter the United States. No security injustice, No girls; call it even. I got out of the airport.

I was feeling very hungry after a long journey; the first signboard I saw was "Subway," so I decided to "eat in United States." I ran to the shop, and it took me quite some time to order the sandwich. There were so many types of cheese, butter, bread, and toppings. I had experience with only one type of sandwich "Band Kabab" in Sukkur (my hometown). Finally I was able to order "something" and the lady on the other side of the counter asked "Here, to go?" This is something I heard for the first time in my life. In Pakistan, we usually say, "Pack it" or "Parcel." I was wondering what she could probably mean, when she asked again, "Sir, Here, to go?"

"Where to go?" – I replied.

"No, I am saying, here to go," she asked again.

"Listen, I don't want to go any where! I am hungry! For God's sake, give me the sandwich!" – I replied.

Now, when I look back, I can't stop laughing!

Then, there was another big shock waiting for me, this time in Melbourne, FL; the "Hurricane." Hurricane is the synonym of "Lantern" in my hometown. I thought it would be some kind of a festival where people light up lanterns or candles to celebrate something. I was quite comfortable until I saw the weather forecast and then I experienced three major hurricanes in one year; Frances, Ivan, and Jeanne. The University campus and housing was closed, and there was no other place to go. I spent those days with an acquaintance at UCF. I was less scared and more excited to witness how Mother Nature harasses the Super Power of the world! By the way, I observed that the hurricanes with feminine names were more devastating than others.

The Coming Weeks

I had a hard time understanding the American accent, especially the African-Americans. To get acquainted with the American way of talking, the idioms, the customs, and especially the humor, I started watching "Friends" and "Sex and the City" on TBS, and this is how I got my third definition of the United States - "**Funny, Sexy and Outspoken.**" The TV shows improved my English, my accent and helped me to understand why Americans laugh at certain things and what the meaning of seemingly innocent sentences is.

During the next few weeks, I learned about pet rights, garage sales, NIMBY, TGIF, Baby Shower, gays and lesbians, Halloween, Thanksgiving, and Santa Claus. As a matter of fact, I received a nice blanket from Santa Claus and I now believe in Santa Claus; thanks Santa, you don't discriminate.

I found the meal times very awkward. In Pakistan, I used to have lunch at 3:00 PM and sometimes as late as 4:30 PM and dinnertime was at 10:00 o'clock. Here, in the States, the lunch begins at 12:30PM and the campus dining center closes at 7:00PM. In the beginning I remained hungry for the first few weeks.

It becomes next to impossible for me to get used to the US cuisine. It doesn't matter which eatery it is; Papa Johns, Mama Foes, Taco Bell or Denny's; I continue to fail to enjoy it.

In my hometown, there is not a single KFC or McDonalds branch. I like my own "Desi food" (an endearing term for Pakistani cuisine), like Korma, Biryani, Zarda, etc. The only thing I like in the United States, and probably can't live without, is Krispy Kreme. It is due to their delicious, and not too healthy, donuts I have managed to gain 40 pounds in one year.

Short term blessings

I found the US blessings brief and awkward compared to Pakistani blessings. Here in America, God is not included in blessings. "Have a nice day", "Have a nice weekend", "Safe journey", "Drive safely", "Take care" seemed very strange as compared to "Have so many children", "Have a long-life", "God will shower His choicest blessings upon you", "You will see the marriage of your grand-grand children", "God will protect you from any danger" etc.

Spare Change

After a week or so, I made the following table to remember the differences between Pakistan and the US:

Pakistan	USA
Signal	Light
Petrol	Gas
High Way	Free Way
Cold Drink	Soda
Right hand drive	Left hand drive
220 Volts	110 Volts
To On: Switch Down	To On: Switch Up
Kilometers	Miles
Celsius	Fahrenheit
Second hand	Pre-Owned
University	School
Biscuit	Cookies
Snaps	Pictures
Divorce	Break-Up
Kilograms	Lbs
dd/mm/yy	mm/dd/yy

University and Professors:

The university that I am enrolled in, Florida Institute of Technology in Melbourne, Florida is very large. The university I graduated from in Pakistan is the size of its library alone. My professors are very nice, always available and we can even have a drink or tea with them; so unbelievable. The hardest part for me (and I am still struggling with it) is to call them by their first names.

The gentleman who heads our department teaches mathematics with the help of pizza, cartoon characters (he likes Sponge Bob and so do I) and encourages two-way communication. In my hometown, I used to be thrown out of my math classes for asking too many questions. Americans are so cool, polished, sophisticated, educated, and civilized with a good sense of humor and respect. My definitions started to change and I couldn't believe it. Every night I had to repeat to myself that I am in the land of the "Kuffar," the land of prejudice and every day tries to prove me absolutely wrong, but, I was not open enough to dispense all of my earlier beliefs.

American Culture – The Reason to Change

The best thing I have found in American culture, which is so unique, is the respect given to all people regardless of their race, sex, age, social and marital status. This is a culture of greetings and instant blessings, every body starts with, "How're you doing?" and ends with "Have a nice day!". When you sneeze, you instantly heard so many voices of "Bless you," When you need help, somebody is always there. If you are in a queue, everybody is in a queue, nobody is superior to you and nobody can cross you on the basis of he or she being a government official or supporter of some political group. Nobody is being categorized by their work or profession. Every body has their own respect. This is the part we are missing in my society back home. We dishonor a person so many times that he could loose his self-respect, which usually affects his sanity.

Another thing is to listen to and recognize others; one can agree or disagree without causing violence. This is one of the first things that I learned from America. People generally are honest and don't lie, even for small things. I don't have the fear of being killed while I'm engaged in praying at mosques in the US. Isn't it ironic, that Islam is safer in the "Land of Kuffar" (Non-Muslims)?

Here comes the fourth definition of America – **"The Land of Justice and Rules."**

Zeeshan-ul-hassan Usmani – Pakistan

The Other Side

While, there are lots of good things in the US culture, there are some bad things too - like in any other culture in the world.

The worst thing I have found in US culture is its family system and family values. I am the youngest of 14 siblings; 9 brothers and 5 sisters. My sisters got married and went to live with their in-laws, while all brothers lived together in a single house (huge house), with their wives and children in something called the joint-family system. I have to make an Excel spreadsheet to keep a record of how many nephews and nieces I have and to identify the parents of each child. Every time I went back to home I had to add one or two more names.

Recently, my eldest brother's daughter became the mother of a lovely baby girl and that makes me a great-uncle at the ripe age of 27! Generally at this age, the average American only begins to think about marriage and here I am, already a great-uncle! I am from a very conservative family system. I was used to children running around the house and all sorts of activities taking place around me. Here in the States, I missed all that liveliness. Here, no one really knows who their next door neighbor is. As soon as children become teenagers, they start to think that they have independent lives and the advice of their parents begins to become obsolete. As soon as they reach the age of 18, they move out, never to come back to their parents' house. Its sad that the rights of pets are more than the rights of parents in this country. Dogs can sleep with you but mother can not enter your room without permission. Thanksgiving becomes the tradition of visiting parents to recall, renew and remember the relationship of love. I cannot absorb the once a year ritual for visiting parents.

Another different aspect of the American culture is the place of women in society. Americans women enjoy much more freedom than women in Sukkur. In my country, the men are responsible for taking care of the food, shelter, clothes and all other expenses, while the women are in charge of houses and bringing up the children, and keeping the house clean and intact. This seems a little weird at first but in my opinion, it's the key to keeping the families together and giving the best children to society.

But, overall USA has a system that works.

A Few More Experiences

There are a lot of experiences that survived my stay in the United States; some are interesting, some are shocking, a few are ugly, and the majority is unforgettable. For example, the most fascinating characteristic of the society is Freedom of Speech. Everybody is allowed to do and say whatever they want to, as far as they are obeying the local law. Americans are proud of their home states and there is an inter-state competition going on everywhere.

Another interesting shock is the term "sue"; it seems like everybody is suing every other person in the United States. Somebody told me that it is not wise to help elderly people to cross the roads; people can sue you in case anything goes wrong since you are not certified in CPR to help them. This is not good when the law hinders you from helping somebody. Maybe I got it wrong but I got scared enough not to offer help.

The next strange thing for me is American humor; I was always puzzled at the way they laugh and what they laugh at. I didn't understand the sex related humor at all.

I am glad to see the "Tableegh" (an Islamic way to preach peace and good moral values to society) work here. It is very common to see them in Pakistan, Rai-Wand is the place in Pakistan, where they all gather together annually (it is like a 3 million people gathering). Nizam-ud-din is doing the same role in India. And I was delighted to attend the same gathering and to meet the similar people here at Kissimmee.

Americans are notorious for their lack of general knowledge. At a birthday party once, my host asked me to show her the picture of our God (Allah in Arabic). Thanks to Afghanistan, people at least know where Pakistan is!

I had the opportunity to attend the Fulbright Conference entitled "Melting Pot" in April 2004 at New York City and I loved it. There were dozens of Fulbrighters from all around the world. They gathered together to melt the pot and further the understanding between the nations. After I attended the conference, I now think about its significance and my educational goals start shifting from Computer Science to world politics, peace and conflict resolutions. And now, I would like to pursue my PhD in political science.

The lessons I learned, and experiences I gained continue to broaden my vision towards the world and its people, the different cultures and the value of mutual understanding. I felt the need: whatever I am learning here in the US is not known to the majority of people in my country, Pakistan; where the literacy rate is only 23% and to be literate means to be able to sign your own name in native alphabets. To extend this understanding I wrote down all of these in the form of a 160 page book in my native language. It was published in December 2005 in Karachi, Pakistan and now I am planning to distribute it as much as I can so that I may help the people understand the Americans and their ways, and so that I can help them change the same definition that I once had of USA before being enriched by the Fulbright program.

After, going through all these experiences, finally I have found the fifth and most appropriate definition of America – **"The Land of Justice, Peace, Friendship, Love, Understanding, Freedom and Opportunity."**

Thank you America

Wait a minute - this is what Islam says - respect others, respect their rights, do not discriminate, live a peaceful life and let others live and do not lie. Are we not considering Quran a 'Read-Only' scripture and Americans are, unknowingly, doing exactly what it says?

Now it's time for a confession: I have to revise my definition about America and its people. They are different in the way they should be; more civilized, peaceful and educated. I have erased every single perceived conception of America. I have slowly begun to form new opinions towards the American way based on personal experiences. I am sorry. I have changed. I have changed a lot, maybe even 180 degrees from where I was before. I have started to like America and its people. I was unable to stop it, and I am sorry, extremely sorry.

But, I have to go back. Go back to my country, where I belong, to educate my people, to improve their definitions and views about the USA, and to teach them the lessons of understanding and mutual benefit that I am learning from my Fulbright experience.

Thank You America. Thank you Americans. Thank you Fulbright.

Signing Off,

Zeeshan-ul-hassan Usmani

zeeshan_ul_hassan@yahoo.com

From "Criminal" to Fulbrighter: in the Land of Spartans

Raymund Espinosa Narag – Philippines

Dear reader: this essay is written in a series of flashbacks. These flashbacks occurred, in the same order as described, when I came to the United States. As I sat in the classrooms and experienced this new country, I couldn't help but think about my past and how an unfortunate event greatly helped me to attain the Fulbright scholarship. I hope this essay will stay with you after you have read it.

I am a Filipino scholar in a foreign land.

I have come to the United States to earn a Master's Degree in Criminal Justice. Through the Fulbright student exchange program, I was sent by my country in order to learn the mechanics of the U.S. police, court, and correctional systems. Thus, I am here to gather best practices, so that perchance, my country could develop models for reforms. As such, I have a gargantuan task on my shoulders.

I was once considered a criminal. I was wrongly accused of a heinous crime I did not commit. I was charged with murder, two counts of frustrated murder and three counts of attempted murder in a fraternity related case in December, 1994. I was pursued by the National Bureau of Investigation, prosecuted in court and detained in Quezon City Jail for six years, nine months and four days, pending the duration of the trial. However, this very wrongful accusation contributed towards the quest for my Fulbright scholarship.

Leaving the comforts of home and the hugs and kisses of my wife and little baby girl, I braced myself for the new environment. I knew it would be a rough and tumbling ride ahead, but I have mission greater than myself. I cannot fail.

Suddenly, I am thrust into one of the biggest campus in the United States— the Michigan State University—land of the Spartans. It has expansive lands, so wide that I have to climb the tallest building just to have a glimpse of it. It has forests, golf courses, farms and gardens. It has numerous buildings that cater to every discipline imaginable— from social sciences to medicine and to other specializations. It is a city of its own— it has its own cinemas, hotels, dairy stores, even a power plant in order to supply its energy needs. And like the ancient city of Sparta, it abounds with cultural activities where sports gladiators fight in its huge stadiums, where actors and actresses play in its theaters and where history comes alive with its well preserved museums. I have never seen such a complicated and sophisticated school before.

I underwent the horrors of detention life. Together with my fellow accused, we were made to live in a room that could ideally accommodate 10 inmates but actually had more than a hundred bodies in it. We were made to subsist in a food allowance of P35 a day, which could barely sustain our flesh. Five of my fellow inmates die every month due to diseases, suffocation and emaciated conditions.

Being in the company of scholars is an achievement on its own. But lo and behold, I have to go through the rites of passage in order to get the "Spartan education." For indeed, the rough and tumble ride is real. I have had my share of pain.

For one, I cannot speak English properly. It is difficult to articulate thoughts and think of the words and to express them at the same time. This is a real challenge for me in the classroom, and coupled with the teaching method where every student can simply "butt in" and express what he wants to say, it becomes interestingly profound. The succeeding events will shed some light.

It was our first discussion day in the Adult Corrections class. I came in prepared and I read all the required (and even the optional) readings. To make sure I understood the topic well, I personally summarized what the authors wanted to say. I was pretty confident: I could articulate at least a sentence or two in class.

The teacher started the ball rolling. As soon as she dropped the first question, a classmate presented an idea. Without raising a hand, another classmate rebutted the idea. Then, another classmate barged in and clarified the previous points, declaring that they were in fact arguing the same thing. But wait, wasn't that supposed to be the role of the teacher? I looked at the teacher to seek some guidance, but she simply let the discussions, with much amusement, flow. I was a little confused: we were supposed to be talking about the theoretical reasons of imprisonment, then someone introduced the issue of race and class in imprisonment, then someone connected it with the experience of minorities who were disproportionately overrepresented in prison, then still another associated it to the Hurricane Katrina in New Orleans where most of the victims where minorities. The discussion was interesting and lively but very fast for me. I was just in the process of thinking what to say, grasping for words that will capture my thoughts. As I was about to raise my hand suddenly, another topic had been introduced. Now we were talking about President Bush and the Federal response. I was frustrated that I could not join the discussions at all. Back home, a teacher inquires and then someone has to be acknowledged first before he or she can respond. And the teacher would rotate around the class, so that everyone can have the chance to give an answer. I gazed at the teacher again, praying for some salvation. This time, with a very adept style, she brought the issue back to its original course, sensing that it had gone off to tangent, but sensibly connecting to the topic that the students had stated. I was able to understand the subject matter. I breathed fresh air. But, lo and behold, as soon as the teacher threw another question, the same cycle repeated itself, with everyone articulating his or her ideas as forcefully and determined as one could be. And every time a classmate shared ideas, our teacher put a black mark in the names in the class roster indicating participation upon which our grades will be based.

The horror of detention life is compounded by the responses of the different actors in the penal system. There developed structures within that made life even more miserable for the lowly inmates— inmates could be subjected to punishments if they break the jail's social code; there is an economic divide which made slaves out of the poor inmates, and a culture of repression where every inmate is forced to simply accept the harsh realities and to complain may mean a loss of one's life or limbs.

I realized I was sitting in class for more than two hours now and my voice was nowhere to be heard. My name slate was white as snow. A grim scenario dawned on me. If I will have a low grade in class participation, then I will equally have a low grade overall. And if I have a low grade in one of my classes, then that will not be a good reflection of being a scholar for which my government spent a lot for my education. I traveled half way around the world leaving my family just to be here; so I must make good. Ah, I must say a word and be part of the discussion.

Mustering enough courage and thinking fast, I was able to finally blurt one quick sentence. This time, we were discussing the conditions in the US Corrections System and whether it was still following a rehabilitation model. Imitating their method, without being acknowledged, I stated, "...the United States spent $49 Billion in 2002 for its correction system which was bigger than my country's total budget for that year, an indication that it still cares to the plight of the prisoners." I delivered it with so much passion that I got the attention of the whole class. My teacher commented: "...well, that is a very good international perspective." I was relieved as I got my black mark in the register.

Far from being bitter about my experience, I made use of my time productively in jail. I organized and taught in the literacy program, I spearheaded the inmate organization towards reformatory goals and enrolled myself in a diploma program offered by the University of the Philippines Distance Education. And believing that I was an academician in the wrong place, I studied the mechanics of jail life— I recorded in my journal the power struggles among the inmate leaders and gangs; I took notes on the intricacies of inmate-management relations and captured on my camera vivid scenes, like an inmate subjected to a disciplinary action called "takal". Being a co-implementer of the programs, I also saw the constraints in resources and challenges in the attitude of the different criminal justice actors. And I reflect on those little details: of why inmates escape, of why riots occur, of why inmates come back in jail, of why educational programs fail, etc. I furiously wrote essays, poems and short stories and submitted these to national dailies hoping that they may have interest in publishing it.

These I did with the conviction that someday, when I will be a free man again, I am going to write about the plight of the thousand detainees languishing in our jails. I believe that there must be a divine reason, why an innocent being like me had to undergo such travails. I consoled myself with the thought, that perhaps, I shall be the spokesperson of the downtrodden and the forgotten.

Thus, even while in jail, I prepared myself to the rigors of academic life— that my incarceration is a unique method of research gathering, called "pakikipamuhay." And that the subjects, my fellow inmates with whom I toil everyday, are the rich supplier of concrete and unaltered data. For I believe, the best proof of innocence is my unbridled quest for knowledge.

I realized that to be a Spartan, one must be assertive in class. One must come in prepared and confident of what he or she has to say. One must express his or her opinions self-assuredly. It is natural for students to challenge what the professors say, and there is no traditional authority where ideas are deemed sacred. Everything is open to debate.

I realized further that this is just a manifestation of the US society's desire for everyone to be heard. They enshrined in their constitution the right to free speech and it is practiced right here in the classroom. No wonder their citizens are empowered and involved. They become self-conscious individuals determined to make their presence felt. It was democracy in substance and in action.

Indeed, I am innocent. Evidence established in court declared that I was not present at the scene of the crime and that I was never part of the fracas. Of course, I was wrongly accused. On February 28, 2002, after emaciating in jail for almost seven years, I was a free man.

Immediately upon release, I boldly presented myself to all concerned agencies which have a stake in the criminal justice system. I told them: I had been a living witness to something profound, a survivor in a social malady that has long been neglected. Please "Hear Ye", so it may not happen again.

Back home, we equally practice free speech. But traditional values say we should defer to authorities, and a teacher, presumably because of advanced education, knows "better" than the students. While debate is equally encouraged, it is always the teacher who has the last say. It promotes "order" in the classroom and dissent is seldom heard. It was democracy in substance but needs more action.

For me, that is the first knowledge I gained with "Spartan education"— where, in its towering buildings and expansive lands, students are gathered to cultivate strong character and to become expressive of their thoughts. They debate and disagree forcefully, in the realm of the ideas, so that the best scheme will come out. And by extension: for the criminal justice system to be effective, the individual voices must be heard— starting in the classrooms.

Thus, I have a model to follow back home. I shall not fail.

naragray@msu.edu

It's Fun to Live Your Dream

Marina Lukanina – Russia

It is incredible to see how events are being carefully weaved in a nice mosaic of our life and to realize that we are actually the ones who have to pull them together. Originally from Moscow, Russia; years back, I would not even have dreamed that someday I will be living in downtown Chicago, pursuing my masters as a Fulbright scholar and going to Mexico City to the International Camping Congress, and most importantly - step-by-step getting closer to my ultimate goal of working in a camp field.

In my opinion there is nothing more interesting and challenging than trying out various paths in life, particularly a path to graduate school. It is a perfect chance to view myself from a distance, to estimate my strengths and weaknesses, to assess my desire for studying, and, finally to clearly realize my career aspirations. Of course the process is rather complex – at every stage you have to sell yourself and your ability, at every stage you are tested – and it requires a lot of self-discipline. "Studying is a demanding process, in process of which we will encounter pain, pleasure, victory, defeat, doubt and happiness," - says Paulo Freire. For this reason, studying requires the development of rigorous discipline, which we must consciously forge in ourselves...we are agents of discipline"[11]. It is amazing how accurately these words could be applied precisely to my graduate studies.

Usually a person decides to enter graduate school a couple of years after he or she has been engaged in a full-time job, after he or she has been "out there, in the real world" applying skills and knowledge acquired during the undergraduate process of studying. When I am to reply to what influenced my decision the most to enroll in graduate school, I am unable to give one answer. I believe that while taking such an important decision, like the continuation of studies on a graduate level, a lot of aspects are usually taken into consideration. I can name a few of them that played a key role in my decision making. Most of all I consider graduate school as a perfect place to combine theory and practice. In my opinion these two things have to be inseparable otherwise they do not make sense.

For me the decision of going to graduate school meant not only changing my working environment but also choosing another country to live at for an extended period of time. It was not an easy decision as I had to quit a good job in Moscow; however I thought that such an opportunity as a Fulbright grant might come by once in a lifetime. I would definitely benefit from whatever brings me closer to my eventual goal, which is getting into a camp sphere on a professional level. It was also a matter of seeing life in a larger perspective rather than making short-term career plans. Everything happens for a reason – events that are happening in our lives are signs and it is only up to us to be able to *read* the signs properly and follow them even if sometimes we cannot know for sure what is

---

[11] I was awarded a Cambridge Commonwealth Trust Scholarship to Cambridge in 2000/2001.
1 Paulo Freire. Don't let the fear of what is difficult paralyze you./ Teachers as Cultural Workers: Letters to those who dare to teach.

waiting for us around the corner. I assume that is when our intuition comes in handy.

What could be a better place that allows a person to stop and think whether this is the type of the career he or she wishes to pursue? To meet lots of new people who are interested in the same field just as much as you? To expand your connections; networking with various organizations related to your field: one of which might even end up being your permanent employer after graduation? The answer to all these questions is the same – graduate school. It gives us a great opportunity to share our objectives and goals with a variety of people. By writing and speaking out our ideas in public we convey them to others. Depending on our oratorical and verbal abilities we may get people excited and inspired in the field we are interested in, which means we will get more people who "think alike" – the ones who will be working in the same direction as we are creating various community organizations (like camps for example). The success of any type of work starts from the right networking and communication. That is something that people acquire at school, in their neighborhoods, while traveling and of course at graduate school.

When I look back upon my life I can easily trace the process of transformation I have gone through since the age of 18. It seems to me that my life is actually divided into 2 parts - before and after 1999. 1999 was the year when I first participated in Camp Counselors USA Program and came to this country along with 1300 other participants to work in American children's camps.

I learned about student exchange program called Camp Counselors USA in 1990 when I was only 9 years old. That year my sister participated in it. I remember very well the excitement in our family associated with her departure. At that time in the USSR, a trip to America was perceived as something unreal and impossible. I was proud to tell all my friends that my sister was going to the United States not just to travel but also to work in one of the American summer camps. I still keep her letters that she sent us from there and like to re-read them once in a while. I was really impressed by one of her lines: "Marina, study English. May you get to see and experience as much as I did". That line got stuck in my memory so much that since then I was looking forward to the time I could take part in this program. Nine years I was patiently (and sometimes impatiently) waiting for the time when I could take part in the program. Meantime I was studying English really hard anticipating that in some years it would be my only way of communication at the US camp. In 1999 the dream of a nine-year old girl came true.

For me that trip to the USA was the first big trip on my own, especially for such a long time. During that orientation meeting I met a girl who was going to the same camp as me. At that time I guess neither of us imagined that this trip would make us best friends, that 4 years later Tanya would move to Moscow and we would work at the same company. Right at the beginning we kind of stuck to each other and later at the camp everyone was very surprised to know we met just one day before we left to camp. It seemed, as we knew each other for a long time.

Recollecting the first week at the camp makes me smile, but at that time I was in a real shock. As I mentioned before it was my first trip abroad on my own and I didn't have caring parents and sister to look after me. Although in a week everything changed. I met so many wonderful people thanks to whom, the summer of 1999 turned out to be actually "the best summer of my life" (CCUSA slogan). The first summer, of course, had a big impact on me, helped me learn about a lot of new aspects about myself and, moreover, gave me an opportunity to meet a lot of interesting people, practice my English and made me think about my future study plans in this country.

Participation in this program, for the most part, has been a major influence on my personality. For four summers I was totally immersed in the international community as the staff and campers came from various parts of the world ranging from Canada to New Zealand. Working at this camp gave me a great opportunity to work and communicate with people from all over the world. It made me realize that international exchange programs in such surroundings as camps are the best means to promote mutual understanding and respect among nations. They provide excellent opportunities for children and adults to get to know other cultures and rediscover their own.

I think that if we are lucky, people we meet on our life road usually enrich and sharpen it in a better way. The role of a mentor is the key element of forming one's personality. I consider myself to be an extremely lucky person as all through my life I have been coming across people, who "leave footprints on our hearts and we are never ever the same again". That was with my high school literature teacher (who taught me how to *read* and by that of course, I, do not mean the mechanical process), the supervisor of my diploma project (who developed the necessary academic and personal qualities in me) and finally a special camp director who basically defined my life-long vocation.

It was highly enriching for my personal and professional development to work under supervision of such camp director as Jay Stager. I consider him to be the most influential person in my life as he showed me the ideal example of an achieving and a goal-oriented person. Seeing this wonderful example of a successful businessman and an outstanding camp director – a person, who has a special talent of working with children, made me think about working in camp sphere and to establish my own International arts camp someday - the Music Camp which will unite professional musicians and amateurs from all over the world through the universal language of music.

Applying for the Fulbright scholarship and getting to Columbia College, Chicago to study youth arts development was another step forward to achieving my goal of getting into the camp sphere. But originally I was placed at the University of New Orleans, so I arrived in Louisiana just 2 weeks prior to the national tragedy: Hurricane Katrina. It was my first visit to the southern part of the USA. It was a dramatic change compared to my summer in Maine. I was willing to experience the unique culture of New Orleans and expand my notion about the USA on the whole, but the circumstances made some changes in my plans.

The news about coming hurricane sounded terrifying. I come from a city that never experiences any type of natural disasters, so even before the New Orleans officials announced the mandatory evacuation my Indonesian roommate, her boyfriend and I jumped into the car and headed to Houston. Two days after, as we watched the news, we could hardly realize what we had managed to escape from. I guess no one expected that Katrina would end up being so devastating. TV reports from New Orleans were just shocking.

There was one day in Houston when I felt complete despair. It seemed to me I was in the middle of nowhere, with a couple of clothes that I took with me since we were sure we would be back in Louisiana within 2-3 days. I had no idea what was going to happen next. But very quickly I understood that panic would not help me and I kept thinking that generally we are given what we can handle. So I put myself together and started to take action. Luckily a Fulbright office was located in Houston and it was one of the first places I went to. Under such grave circumstances I met my Fulbright officer Marie Ward. It should be especially noted that she is a wonderful person! I was completely lost when I came to her for the first time; I did not have any clear picture of the future. But thanks to her efficient support and dedication I was among the first ones who were placed into a new university. I will also be grateful to Arthur Austin, Senior World Area Manager, Europe from IIE, NY office, who helped a lot with getting me to Chicago. That is how I got to study at Columbia College.

When I got on the plane heading from Houston to Chicago I could not help but experience a feeling of relief. The notion that I am going to the mid-west was so comforting. Even though I have never been to Chicago before, and I knew no one there, I was taking it as a new and exciting challenge in my life. As I got here, I was lucky once more to be encircled by very nice and helpful people starting from my Fulbright officers Christina Holdvogt and Megan Spillman to my graduate school admission director Becky Snyder and associate chair of my department Phyllis Johnson. Right from the beginning I felt so welcome that I did not have any adaptation period here. Very soon Chicago became "my town".

"Every person, all the events of your life, are there because you have drawn them there. What you choose to do with them is up to you", said one of my favorite writers Richard Bach in his immortal book "Illusions, The Adventures of a Reluctant Messiah"".

Unfortunately we can't always explain and see the reasons of the negative events in our lives. And it's impossible that only good and happy events happen in our lives. One of the most difficult things that a person should learn is to accept all the events that are happening through his or her life path (whether they are positive or negative) and be able to get as much positive possible from them. My experience of dramatic change during the first weeks of my Fulbright program proved that.

Shortly after moving to Chicago I was able to attend two events that were educationally extremely enriching and motivating. Both events have absolutely different scales, however, both of them served as additional proof for me that I am on the right path, that precisely in such an environment as a camp, where I want to develop my future career. These events were International Camping Congress in Mexico City (organized by International Camping Fellowship, hosted by Mexican Camping Association), October 2005 and Student Camp Leadership Academy - pilot program offered by American Camp Association first week-end of November in Illinois. I was the only one from the participating side that managed to attend both events.

It is hard to think of a better place for an International Camping Congress than Mexico; a country with a rich culture, great people, and a totally fascinating atmosphere. I guess I won't be able to judge this Congress objectively as it was the first ICF Congress that I attended and in the country. I have always felt very special about. Yet I truly believe it was especially enriching for young professionals who have only begun to make their first steps in the camp management career. It was an excellent opportunity to meet and communicate with camp gurus as well as mixing with Mexican counselors; learning how things are done in another country. Visiting Mexican camps and talking to Mexican camp directors was an invaluable experience.

When I heard about an opportunity to participate in Student Camp Leadership Academy from American Camp Association Executive Director of Illinois Section Gordon Kaplan I got really excited. Something I have never heard before – a Camp Academy! Reading the SCLA's goals in the Internet I was a bit skeptical. Usually when you read mission statements of various organizations or projects, they all tend to have ambitious goals and SCLA was not an exception. I wondered how such complex goals could be accomplished in just one weekend. I would say the SCLA definitely has outgrown its own goals it originally had. By getting together with 11 more participants and 8 professional staff I felt being part of starting something very important. The event was especially precious in terms of introducing young people who only start their "camp career path" to the actual job of a camp director, of all the aspects this profession is about.

"It's fun to live your dream", as one of my familiar camp directors once said. I would say without exaggeration that Fulbright is definitely helping me live my dream – to study and expand my knowledge, to acquire invaluable experience of meeting and to communicate with lots of different people. Fulbright provides significant positive influence on a one's development by giving one a chance of celebrating one's difference. We will have the chance to make future generations more perceptive and flexible. They will come to understand the necessity to learn and respect the differences in our diverse and fast-moving world. I view the Fulbright program as bridging mutual understanding and friendship among nations.

Pursing a master's or PhD degree is challenging yet extremely interesting and rewarding. So difficulties should be viewed as opportunities, possible failures as the way to success. And most importantly, always remember that "you are never given a wish without being given the power to make it come true. You may have to work for it, however.""[12]

moosehead_marina@yahoo.com

---

[12] Richard Bach. Illusions, The Adventures of Reluctant Messiah

The Odyssey of a Fulbrighter

Louis-Marie Ngamassi Tchouakeu
- Cameroon

I. Pre-Academic Experience in Athens, Ohio

Through its office of Educational and Cultural Affairs, the US Embassy in Yaounde (Cameroon) regularly organizes award contests for various exchange programs. I was one of the laureates of the 2001/2002 Fulbright Fellow Enhancement contest, to enroll in a graduate program in Information Systems in the US. Having French as a first language, I had to undergo an English language training prior to the academic course. This pre-academic program took place at Ohio University in Athens, Ohio and lasted eight months (January 7 to August 27, 2002).

The News

It was with mixed feelings I learned that I was awarded the Fulbright Enhancement Fellowship. On the one hand, I was sad because I was suddenly going to leave my family for almost three years. I was also sad because I had insufficient time to get ready. In fact, I barely had one month between the date I was informed about the award, 12/4/01, and the departure date, 1/3/02. That period was too short for an appropriate preparation for such a long journey. This may explain why I was homesick during my entire first month in the United States, yet I was very happy with the award at the same time. Having been chosen for the highly selective Fulbright award on my first attempt was a motive for personal pride. I was also very happy for my family, especially my children. Since they attend an Anglophone school in Cameroon, I would have the opportunity to learn more about the Anglophone system of education and could then provide more effective advice to them. Finally, I was very happy for my university. My award was going to end years of misfortune. For a long while, no candidate from the University of Dschang had been successful in obtaining the Fulbright award. Moreover, I sincerely believed that upon completion of the program, I would contribute significantly to the improvement of the overall management of my institution through the latest knowledge of Computer based Information Systems. All this joy gave me enough strength to overcome my sadness and prepared me for the challenges that I knew I was going to face.

The Shock

I left Cameroon on January 3, 2002, for Athens, Ohio, the hometown of Ohio University. The first thing that struck me on my arrival was the cold weather. The difference in the temperature between my country and my new place of residence was stark. I went from a suffocating hot dry season in Douala (over 100° F) to a freezing winter in Athens (less than 20° F). During the first weeks, I experienced a lot of difficulty adjusting to the brutal change in temperature. Fortunately, I was welcomed very warmly by the Ohio Program of Intensive English (OPIE). They had arranged for a room in a dorm (Scott Quad) not far from the classroom (less than 100m). I would "jump" from the dorm to the class and vice-versa. Apart from the weather, I also experienced several cultural and environmental differences such as food, habits, music, clothing, and the social behavior etc. But I got acquainted with these differences within a short period of time.

The Challenge

At the beginning of the pre-academic program, my challenge was not so much to learn the English language but to learn how to be a student again. I had stopped being a regular student decade ago, and since then things had changed a lot, especially in the field of Information Technology. So, the idea that I was going to sit for hours in a class taking notes and doing assignments was a bit scary. But I did it. In the beginning it was difficult, but in the end everything went smoothly.

Friends

The friends I made during my eight month stay in Athens helped improve my oral communication skills very much. The OPIE "Conversation Partner" program gave me the first opportunity. My conversation partner took me around the university campus and presented me with the major facilities such as the impressive OPIE Language Resource Center, the library, the Computer Service Center, the Health Center and Ping Recreation Center. At each of these facilities, he would explain to me how to utilize them. My conversation partner also took me around Athens (uptown, Athens Mall, University Mall) and its surroundings (Athens County old coal mines). Apart from my conversation partner, I was good friends with almost all my classmates at OPIE. In my academic classes, only those with whom I was involved in team work were close to me. Others were not patient enough to hold a long conversation with me due to my accent. I was also friends with nearly all my teachers. My active participation in class brought them very close to me. I also made some friends through the church. During my stay, I practiced my Catholic faith as an active member of the St. Paul Parish community, and that is how I came to learn more about some social issues, such as the importance given to children's rights in the US. The fact that all of these friends could only speak English with me helped me improve my language skills. In eight months, I had set up a solid relationship network in the University milieu and around the town of Athens, so much so that it is with pain that I left Athens.

The Dorm

Life in the dorm was enjoyable. My room was well furnished (bed, desk, chair, computer, printer, access to the Internet, cable TV). My roommate, an undergraduate American, was very nice. At the beginning, we had a lot of problems in communication. He spoke very fast, and I could hardly understand. But he made an effort to slow the pace and in the long run we overcame our problem. My roommate introduced me to most of his friends and some family members, and every time he would encourage them to speak with me. We would spend a whole weekend night talking about differences and similarities in African and US culture. Soccer was another interesting topic of conversation. I took the example of the 2002 World Cup soccer tournament in Japan and Korea to talk about sports in Africa in general and Cameroon in particular.

Campus Life

I participated in many ways in campus life during my stay. I was not only a good "consumer" of events organized on the campus, but also an actor. I was an active member of two student associations: the African Student Union and the Ohio University Fulbright Scholars Association. Although nominated for many elected positions in the executive board of the African Student Union, I did not run for the elections because I knew I would not stay in Athens. During Ohio University International Week, I took part in the organization of the annual International Street Fair, in which I presented some aspects of Cameroonian culture through traditional clothing. As another contribution to campus life, I gave a talk in French in a Linguistics class as guest speaker. The topic was "French Speaking Countries in Africa". This was another opportunity for me to talk about Africa, but this time in French and to a specific audience. All sixteen students of the class were present and were very eager to learn. I could tell by the attention they paid while listening to me and the number of questions they had prepared. Within an hour, I had answered more than forty questions. In the feedback to their teacher, all the students were very satisfied with the talk and expressed the wish to invite me once more. Unfortunately, due to time constraints, that wish could not be satisfied. Finally, as a member of the OPIE student representative board, I contributed to the improvement of services for students. I also wrote an article for "The OPIE ZONE", the OPIE newsletter.

Recreation

Fishing was one of my favorite recreational activities. I went fishing with classmates and some of my teachers several times. It was fun! I also cherished playing ping pong but did not always have the opportunity to have someone to play with.

Language Learning

I used both formal and informal learning methods to improve my English language skills.

Formal:

I attended all the classes regularly and was always on time. I remember that I came late once. That was due to the summer time change. I also made every effort to complete all assignments and turned them in on time. Finally, I participated very actively in class, by volunteering to answer questions, by asking for clarification on matters I did not understand and by giving presentations on various topics, such as the influence of language in Cameroon culture, the problem of underage workers in Cameroon, higher education in Cameroon, the Information Systems of the University of Dschang, food culture in Cameroon.

Informal:

TV and radio programs, the library, the OPIE Learning Resource Center and friends were instrumental to my learning process in an informal way. TV and radio programs helped me to improve my listening comprehension skills. Every day, I would sit for hours, listening to the radio or watching television. My favorite radio station was NPR. "The Golden Girls," "The Cosby Show" and "The People's Court" were some of the TV programs I enjoyed the most. In addition to those two media sources, I visited the library very often to read and to use the computer services (free printing). I also spent most of my time in the OPIE Learning Resource Center. These two facilities helped me to improve my reading and my pronunciation skills. It was therefore with no surprise that I earned full credit for all OPIE classes and did pretty well in my academic classes, earning two grades of "A+" and one "A-".

The Classes

During my stay, I took a total of ten classes: seven OPIE classes (CS2, Mythology, Grammar, Graduate Writing, Oral Communication I and II, and Ecology and Environment) and three undergraduate academic classes (Business Information Systems (BIS) and VB Programming at the College of Business and Programming in C at the school of Computer Science). I think that I did the best I could in all of them. The purpose for taking academic classes was to improve my language skills in the field of my major. Here I learned a lot from my teachers but also from classmates through team projects. With my long working experience, I contributed a lot to team work, mostly in the BIS class.

OU – UDS Cooperation

During my stay, I made some important contact in view of possible future cooperation between my institution, The University of Dschang and Ohio University. As a matter of fact, I met with the

Director of the Institute for the African Child, W. Stephen Howard, with whom I talked about projects through the African Studies Program. I also met with Gerard A. Akindes, in charge of one of the computer labs (Grover) of Ohio University. We envisaged projects in the domain of transfer of technology from the US to Africa.

My Judgment

My overall appreciation of the pre-academic program is very good. This program was well organized and implemented from the beginning to the end. All the courses I took met my expectations. Moreover, all the teachers were very experienced and always available when needed for help. There was a good balance between classes and outdoor activities. The teaching resources were varied and adequately used. The monthly test system for the GRE and TOEFL set up by IIE was a bit stressful but turned out to be very helpful. This system kept us constantly focused on our training. Although I had achieved the minimum score required by IIE on the TOEFL test in my first try, I remained under pressure until the month of May when I was happy to learn that I was not required to take the test any more. The small and quiet town of Athens served as a good catalyst for my studies.

Acknowledgment

During my stay at Ohio University, I got sufficiently good help and care from both IIE and the OPIE staff. Andreea Mercean, my contact at IIE, was really very close to me during the whole program. She did tremendous job counseling, advising, and providing me with necessary information when needed. In general, I found all the OPIE staff very helpful. They seemed to fully understand the problems of international students (much more than the people at the International Students Office at OU). I was treated very nicely by all at the OPIE office. I often felt as if I was given special care. As my core class teacher and my OPIE adviser, Mr. John Bagnole contributed a lot to the improvement of my English language skills. I appreciate the tremendous effort he made to enroll me in the appropriate academic classes. Dawn Rogier, Susan Gould and Greg Kessler were more friends than teachers. They took good care of me, not only with class-related problems but also, with personal problems.

Mr. Patrick Miller, my "special" personal adviser, was the person with whom I felt the most comfortable. I would turn to him first when I needed any kind of help. He was always available and ready to help. John McVicker and Cynthia Holliday also contributed a lot to my training. Finally, the staff at the office of Educational and Cultural Affairs at the US Embassy in Yaounde, especially Mr. Gerald Chilla, deserves a word of thanks. They made the necessary arrangements prior to my arrival in the United States.

Conclusion

This account of my Fulbright orientation program is largely positive. Time has passed so quickly, and it is hard to believe that I have spent eight months in the United States. The logical explanation of this is that the training program was so intense and exciting that I could not see the time pass. This pre-academic program was a very enriching experience. I feel I have learned a lot and have also contributed a lot through my active participation in the program, especially by sharing my experience about African culture. My wish is to see some of the contacts that I have initiated here lead to cooperation between Ohio University and The University of Dschang. As a result of these links, other Cameroonians will also have the opportunity to benefit from the important human and material resources of Ohio University. Otherwise, it is with great optimism that I am looking forward to starting my academic program at Pace University, New York City.

II. Academic Experience in New York City

From Athens (Ohio) to New York City

At the end of my pre-academic program, I learned with great joy and excitement that I was admitted to Pace, a University in New York City. I was going to move from Athens, a small university town to one of the biggest cities in the world. My dream to live in New York was becoming a reality. After spending time in Paris (1983 to 1985), I was going to experience life in another big city. I was also going to do my academic program in an environment where I could easily experience the latest information technologies. Moreover, moving to New York was taking me closer to a bigger Cameroonian community. There were just two Cameroonians in Athens and we missed the warmth of our country.

Before my placement at Pace University by the Institute of International Education (IIE), I knew nothing about the school. After a Google search, two things drew my attention. First, the President of Pace, Dr. David A. Caputo was a Fulbrighter; I felt proud of myself once more. Second, the Pace University downtown campus where I was admitted, was just a few blocks from the World Trade Centre, the 9/11 terrorist attack site. The fact that I was going to see for myself the scene of this historic tragedy thrilled me. I also learned about the University motto, "opportunitas" and committed myself to spare no opportunity to learn as much as possible at Pace.

Settling in New York City

Obtaining an apartment in New York was a real nightmare. From Athens, I went to visit one of my relatives in Boston. It was from there that I started to look for a place to live in New York. I made hundreds of phone calls in response to ads, sent messages to the Fulbright listserv, and contacted all the people I knew could help. I also made several round trips from Boston to New York to visit some apartments. Most of them were too expensive (over $1000).

Those that were affordable were in areas I was advised to avoid (e.g. Harlem). I was at the edge of despair when, on the eve of school's reopening date, I got a place in Brooklyn (Church Avenue and Nostrand Avenue). I was going to share with a fellow Cameroonian, an apartment located 40 minutes by subway from the school.

New York City was very different from Athens. The thing that struck me the most on my arrival was the size: gigantic. It took more than three months to develop a basic understanding of the geography of the city and the different transportation systems (subway, taxi, bus, train etc.). Going out alone really scared me in the beginning. I remember that I arrived more than one hour late for the first appointment that I had at IIE for my orientation session. I had missed my transfer and gotten confused in the subway. Later, however, I quickly became more confident about getting around in the city. A Metropolitan Transit Authority (MTA) map of NYC was always in my wallet. New York City was also a very cosmopolitan and busy place compared to Athens. On the street, you would meet people of very different origins. Businesses were open 24/7. You could go shopping at your convenience. My favorite shopping place was 32nd street, between 4th and 6th Avenue. There, I would bargain as we do in Cameroon.

Joining Haut-Nkam New York Association

I joined the Haut-Nkam New York Association barely one month after setting in New York. Haut-Nkam is one of the 58 administrative divisions of Cameroon. It is also my place of origin. Haut-Nkam had a very active community in New York with more than a hundred people. We had learned, while growing up in Cameroon, that together we stand, divided we fall, especially in a foreign country. This was the spirit that led to the creation of the association Haut-Nkam New York in the year 2000.

Pace Downtown Campus

Pace University's Downtown campus had very little in common with Ohio University's campus in Athens. While the Athens campus was big and covered nearly the whole town; in New York, everything was concentrated within a few buildings at a walking distance. In terms of number of students, OU had more than twice as many as Pace—an estimated 33,000 at OU versus about 14,000 at Pace. Security on campus was more rigorous at Pace. Wearing the school badge was mandatory. The terrorist attack was still very fresh in most people's memories. The Pace community had lost some of its members during the tragic event.

Study objective in the US

As I mentioned earlier, I was awarded the Fulbright scholarship for a Master's degree in Information Systems. Prior to the award, I was working as Head of the Computer Division at the University of Dschang, one of the six state-owned Institutions of Higher Learning in Cameroon. I had held the position for almost a decade and had experienced certain problems I thought further training could help to solve. A waste of resources due to poor information management systems was severely undermining the activities of the University. Data was stored in multiple, separate databases, leading to very high data redundancy and inconsistency. Computers were mainly used for word-processing. Moreover, key management software packages (academic affairs, financial management) were contracted out and the University found itself quite often taken hostage by private software makers who were unavailable when needed for urgent interventions. In addition to all this, the University also suffered from poor communication technology facilities. For example, Internet access was through a dial-up connection and overall, they could count just about one computer for 100 students. The university community (over 400 full-time academic staff, 500 support staff and an estimated 10,000 students) was almost cut off from the rest of the world, and we were experiencing a lot of problems accessing scientific and technical information and publishing research.

My Fulbright training was intended to help find solutions to these problems. Upon completion of the program, I was expected to contribute to the set up of an efficient computer-based information management system at the University that would generate timely and accurate data for decision making. I was also expected during my program, to have created networks, made contacts and created relationships that could help to somewhat relieve the isolation of Dschang University.

Pace's School of Computer Science and Information Systems

I did my Master's degree at Pace's School of Computer Science and Information Systems (SCSIS). SCSIS was in a brand new building located at 163 Williams Street in Manhattan. The classrooms were equipped with the latest teaching technologies. Unlike in Athens, all my classes were scheduled in the evening. I had enough time during the day to prepare for my lessons. I was very frequently in the library and the computer lab. Most of my classmates were either part-time or full-time workers or most of them were in the IT field. Their real-world experience was very valuable during class and especially in choosing and implementing group projects. Class sizes were good, with 25-30 students maximum. There was also a good balance of international students. The good working environment at the SCSIS motivated me to do the best I could to learn. I also realized how universities in Cameroon in general and the Dschang University in particular were far behind in terms of learning facilities.

With regard to teaching, I very much enjoyed the invitation of IT professionals as outside speakers in some courses, especially in IS Project Management (IS-637) and in the IS Research Seminar (IS-692). I particularly learned a lot from the talk of Liz Hamburg (BEELINE Cellular Communications) during an IS Project Management class. Her presentation was titled "International Project Management: Case study of Voice Mail System into Russian Cellular Network." Another outside speaker that impressed me very much was Michelle McKelvey, Academic Developer Evangelist, Microsoft Education. Her presentation on the Microsoft .NET software was very informative.

I took 44 credits instead of the 36 required for the MS degree. The extra credits were voluntary taken to refresh and update my knowledge in these disciplines and also to start preparing me for my Ph.D. program. The class I enjoyed the most was the software engineering class (CS-615). I had developed, in my long career in software development the bad habit of going directly from the analysis of the problem to coding without proper documentation for the analysis and design phases. Dr Olly Gotel, my software engineering teacher, succeeded in correcting this problem. She stressed the importance of documenting any piece of work and provided helpful standard document templates.

GRADER project

During my Fulbright academic program, I got involved in a research project initiated by Parfait Eloundou-Enyegue, a faculty member at Cornell University. The main objective of the project was to develop a web-based simulation tool for education policy analysis in Africa. As a matter of fact, if African countries are to meet the UN "Millennium Development" targets in the education sector, they must implement highly efficient policies. Identifying the best policies requires reliable tools for appraising beforehand how different policies will likely affect national education outcomes. My role in this project was to design software that education planners could use to simulate beforehand the impact of complex education policies on the schooling outcomes of their country. The project is currently underway.

NABU-Cameroon

My interest in Information and Communication Technology for Development (ICT4D) was intensified at Pace. I took an interesting class taught by Professor Dennis Anderson and titled "Information Systems Research Seminar" during which the problem of the digital divide was debated at length. This class shed more light on this crucial issue and bolstered my determination to help my country and especially my University. As a result, I volunteered in "Knowledge Transfer Beyond Boundaries" (NABU), a non-profit and non-governmental New York-based organization, and launched within the framework of this initiative a project to fight against HIV/AIDS in Cameroon, using ICTs. This project is called NABU-Cameroon Rural Hope Initiative – NABU-CRHI (http://csis.pace.edu/~anderson/Project-NABU/Cameroon/). NABU was founded in 2003 by Professor Dennis Anderson, my academic adviser, and Associate Dean of the School of Computer Science and Information Systems. He is also a Fulbright Senior Specialist in information technology on the roster of the J. William Fulbright Foreign Scholarship Board for the period 2002-2006. Another founding member of NABU was Dr. Joann Halpern, Global Director of Academic and Student Affairs at Long Island University.

The goal of NABU is to contribute (1) to the world effort to reduce, if not close the gap between the "haves" and the "have-nots" and (2) to achieve the Millennium Development Goals. The guiding principle behind NABU's commitment to sustainable development is the implementation of distance education to reach and interact with ethnically and geographically diverse populations.

The NABU-Cameroon project was NABU's pioneer project. In Cameroon, the HIV/AIDS pandemic is growing, especially among the nation's youth. Two of the obstacles to HIV/AIDS prevention in the country are (1) the cultural taboo of talking about sex in public; (2) the lack of sufficient information regarding the dangers of HIV/AIDS, especially in rural areas. NABU-CRHI is prepared to address both of these problems in a unique way. It will utilize the anonymity and availability of information provided by the Internet to deliver HIV/AIDS education to a particular segment of the Cameroon population: university communities. Simultaneously, NABU-CRHI will provide computer education to the members of university communities. This dual focus of NABU-CRHI will improve computer literacy while curtailing the spread of HIV/AIDS in an area of the world whose economy has been devastated by the spread of this debilitating disease. The work on NABU-Cameroon was presented at the 2005 Annual Conference for Comparative International Education Society (CIES 2005) and also at the 2005

NAFSA conference in Seattle. I foresee a "NABU Technology Center" on Dschang University campus by the year 2015.

Beyond the Classroom: Becoming a True New Yorker

Thanks to Metro International, I became a true New Yorker. Metro International is a private NGO that works in New York to create positive relationships among people of different origins and to contribute to making the world a better place to live in. I was very fortunate to learn about Metro International as soon as I arrived in New York. Sarah Wilcox, my adviser at IIE, gave me the information and encouraged me to participate in Metro's programs. Metro's activities target the estimated 50,000 international students and scholars that are in New York area. Metro considers these people to be tremendous resources to promote global learning. Metro is also officially designated to coordinate Fulbright student and scholar enrichment programs in New York City.

Global Classroom

Global Classroom is a program through which Metro International brings international students and scholars into schools to make interactive curriculum-related presentations about their country/culture or area of expertise to elementary/secondary students and educators in New York City.

I participated actively in this program. I gave more than 15 classroom presentations in secondary schools in New York, including EBC Bush wick High School, Legacy High School, and Richmond Hill High School. I talked about the colonization of Africa, the African French speaking countries (colonial history, facts and some aspects of the socio-cultural life), the long-lasting border conflict between Cameroon and Nigeria, the Bakassi peninsula conflict. During one of my presentations, a 12 year-old boy impressed me with a question. He asked me if Africa was ever compensated for all the damages suffered during the colonization. He seemed very disappointed when I gave him a negative answer. Another thing I learned from my involvement in Metro's Global Classroom program was that Cameroon's national soccer team, "Les Lions Indomptables," was the most important ambassador for the country. Whenever I presented myself and said that I was from Cameroon, immediately they would start talking about soccer, the Indomitable Lions and Roger Milla. In addition to giving presentations, I also contributed to Metro's Global Classroom program by serving as a trainer for new Global Classroom speakers.

Open Forum

Metro's Open Forum programs provide opportunities for international students and scholars to discuss on the world's burning issues such as HIV/AIDS, terrorism, insecurity, famine, poverty, etc.

I participated in Metro's open forum program on a regular basis. The forum I enjoyed the most was on the theme "Exploring the Roles & Responsibilities of Global Citizens in a World of Conflict." Topics such as "the role of the United Nations," "sharing world resources," "the American Media's Simplification and Misinterpretation of Outside Issues," "Justice in the World: Responsibilities of Rich Countries in the Development of Poor Countries", were debated by over one hundred participants. I played the role of the convener on the topic "Sharing world resources". The conclusion we came to at the end of our discussion was that the uneven distribution of world resources was also a cause of tension and war in the world. I also participated in a special Fulbright symposium to discuss the challenges and opportunities for global learning in the United States. This event was designed as part of an initiative to encourage dialogue about global issues. Mrs. Harriet Mayor Fulbright was among the panelists.

I also took active part to the events marking the celebration of the Black History Month in February 2003 and February 2004.

This was an opportunity to learn more about the struggle of African Americans for their civil rights.

Community visit

Metro's Community Visits offer participants an opportunity to spend time—one day or a full weekend—with an American host family and experience American life and culture. In turn, participants share their country & culture with American families. Through this program, I spent a Thanksgiving Day with a family in the heart of Manhattan, just a few blocks from the World Trade Centre. I also spent a day in New Jersey (Ho-Ho-Kus) with the Keene family.

Metro-walks

Metro-walks are a great way to meet other students from around the world, make new friends and explore New York City's many hidden corners. This program gave me the opportunity to discover New York's Central Park. It was also through this program that I visited the United Nations Headquarters for the first time.

Fulbright Awards Dinner

Metro's Fulbright Awards Dinner program aims to contribute to raising awareness of the Fulbright program and its role in furthering peaceful relationships between peoples and cultures. During the yearly event, selected people who, in the spirit of Senator J. William Fulbright, have furthered peace and international understanding through their lives and work are honored.

In May 2003, Metro International hosted its 13th annual Fulbright Awards Dinner at the United Nations. This edition was very special to me because I was among those who were chosen to present the awards. The other presenters were: Mrs. Harriet Mayor Fulbright; Paulo Sergio Da Silva, Fulbright from Brazil; and Savera Aslam, Fulbright from Pakistan. Four individuals were honored : Robert J.

Brennan (President and CEO, American Institute for Foreign Study), Thomas S. Johnson (Chairman and CEO, GreenPoint Financial), Lorin Maazel (Music Director, New York Philharmonic), and Violy McCausland-Seve (Founder and President, Violy & Company).

In my remarks, I was grateful to the Fulbright program for the great opportunity I was given to come to the US to further my education. I also talked about my family (2nd in a family of 16; married and father of 3), my culture (food, dance, faith, clothing, sport etc.) and my country (Cameroon: Africa in miniature, peaceful country, hot all year round, severe economic crises, unemployment among youth, alarming growing rate of HIV/AID). After my remarks, many people were curious to know more about me. That is how I met and befriended a lot of people. This event was the greatest opportunity I had ever had to speak in such a very selective milieu and to an important audience. The event marked an important turning point for the rest on my stay in New York. I will never give enough thanks to Margaret Shiba, Executive Director of Metro International and Susan Hackett-Noori, Director of Global Classroom, for giving me the opportunity.

Hundred of Miles covered

During my Fulbright program, I traveled a lot. I went to at least one town in almost every state on the East Coast. I spent a Mardi Gras in New Orleans, Louisiana. I also spent Christmas in West Palm Beach, Florida invited by Mitch Flinchum, a long time friend with whom I worked at USAID in Cameroon. I went several times to Ithaca, NY to visit and work with Parfait Eloundou-Enyegue, a faculty member at Cornell University and a friend and ex-colleague at the University of Dschang. I was also very frequently in Boston to visit my sister, Collette Pungwe. She was a big source of inspiration to me throughout my stay in the US. I also went several times to Detroit to visit Mougoue Mbodja, a cousin of mine who teaches at Wayne State University. I went to Ann Arbor to visit Pat and Ellen Vaughan, the parents of Kelley, a Peace Corps Volunteer I hosted in Cameroon. The Fulbright enrichment program gave me the opportunity to go to the West Coast. I enjoyed the four day stay in San Francisco and the field trip to Menlo Park, Silicon Valley at the Sun Microsystems headquarters.

Other major places I visited include: Columbus OH, Cincinnati OH, Washington DC, Maryland MD, etc....

Meeting High Profile VIPs

My Fulbright program in New York City, the headquarters of the United Nations, gave me the opportunity to meet and converse with certain people I would have never thought I could approach in my lifetime.

First and foremost, I met several times with Mrs. Fulbright. There were four of us who presented the 2003 awards to Metro International's honorees at their annual Fulbright Awards Dinner. We met again the following year at the same ceremony. Before that, we had been together at a couple of events including a symposium organized at New York University (NYU) by Metro International on the theme "Critical Thinking in Critical Times: Challenges and Opportunities for Global Learning in the United States." It was here that I had the opportunity to converse with her for quite a long time without interruption. We talked about her initiatives towards Africa. I remembered she told me she had been in only a few African countries so far but had plans to visit more. We also talked about my NABU-Cameroon project and I expressed the wish that this project could be a reason for her to come to Cameroon.

Secondly, I met with Shanabi from Iraq. The US-led war on Iraq had already begun. He was then president of the Iraqi interim government. This was during the event of the 2003 IIE Annual Awards Dinner at the Plaza Hotel, located on 5th Avenue between 58th and 59th Streets. I was one of the few Fulbright students invited and was fortunate to be seated just a table away from Shanabi. I would have liked to engage in further conversation with him, but his impressive looking bodyguard dissuaded me.

During the same dinner, I met with Robert E. Lewis, Senior Vice President - Chief Credit Officer, American International Group, Inc. He would later become one of the best friends I made during my stay in the US. I will never forget the several opportunities he gave me to discuss IT-related issues with his IT colleagues, namely Lou Amato, Maria Berenguer and Allan Hackney. We discussed among other topics, some perspectives of how major financial institutions in the US address their IT challenges. He also offered me to have the best view I ever had of New York from the top of their building (70 Pine Street in Manhattan). His advice for solving some of the problems we were facing at the University of Dschang and his encouragement for the launching of the NABU-Cameroon Project were very much appreciated.

I also met and enjoyed conversing with Alexandre de Lesseps. In our history book in primary school, we had learned about his great-great-grandfather, the French diplomat Ferdinand de Lesseps, who supervised construction of the Suez Canal in 1879 and presented the Statue of Liberty to the United States in 1886.

Lewis Tucker, Vice President, Internet Services, Sun Microsystems also figures among the special people I met during my stay. This was during the 2003 Fulbright enhancement seminar in San Francisco. A visit to the headquarters of Sun Microsystems at Menlo Park, Silicon Valley was on the agenda of this seminar. Lewis talked about his corporate vision and strategy and also about technology in the next 20 years.

I was also very privileged to count in several occasions among the guest of Dr. Caputo, President of Pace University. This was how I came to meet and converse with a good number of members of Pace University Board of Trustees.

The other people I was fortunate to meet and still remember include:

- Allan E. Goodman, President and CEO, Institute of International Education New York;
- Elise van Oss, President of the Greater New York Fulbright Association Chapter;
- Chancellor Joel Klein of the New York Department of Education.
- Tom Johnson, Chairman and CEO, GreenPoint Financial Bank;
- Gail Schoettler, speaker and international writer on the politics of globalization, political strategies for businesses and women's issues;
- Michael Chertok, co-founder and Managing Director of Global Catalyst Foundation.

Acknowledgment

I would like to express my gratitude for their support to:

My teachers and friends at Pace University, New York University, and Cornell University especially Dennis Anderson, Olly Gotel, Parfait Eloundou, Joann Halpern, Robert Whelan and Kadri Sirg;

The staff of Metro International especially Margaret Shiba and Susan Hackett-Noori;

The staff of Institute of International Education especially Sarah Ilchman;

All the numerous friends I made during my stay in New York;

Special thanks to my Sister Collette Pungwe.

Conclusion

To conclude, I would once more say I was very fortunate to be awarded the Fulbright grant and also to be placed in New York for my academic program. I used this opportunity to learn the best I could and now committed to give back to my country and especially to the University of Dschang, all what I have learned. I also felt I had contributed the best I could, through my active participation in socio-cultural events in New York, to perpetuate the spirit of Senator J. William Fulbright to make the world a better place to live in.

III. Post Academic Experience in Addis Ababa, Ethiopia

I was one of the ten laureates selected in the second edition (2004) of the United Nations Fulbright Fellowship program for a six-month academic training at the United Nations (UN). I joined the Information and Communication Technologies (ICTs) team, Development Information Services Division (DISD) of the Economic Commission for Africa (ECA)[13] in Addis Ababa (Ethiopia) from June 18th, 2004 to December 10th, 2004.

The activities of the DISD ICTs team focused on the implementation of the African Information Society Initiative (AISI), an action framework that had been the basis for information and communication activities in Africa since 1996. AISI's major activities and objectives included the development of national ICT policies and strategies, and building Africa's information and communication infrastructure and capacity involving all major stakeholders.

Getting started

I arrived in Addis Ababa on June 18th and was warmly welcomed at the DISD. I was the first United Nations Fulbright Fellow to come to ECA and it was my first visit to Ethiopia. My first impressions about the DISD, ECA and Addis as a whole were very good.

The working environment was excellent at the DISD. My orientation session gave me the opportunity to meet with the majority

---

[13] http://www.uneca.org/

of the staff of the division. At the end of this orientation I knew I was joining a group of very open-minded and hardworking people.

My Participation

I worked under the supervision of Aida Opoku-Mensah, the ICTs team leader. My original assignment, "research on Open-source and e-government, aimed at providing Public Administration with a unified and flexible Internet database and an application for organizing cooperative work practices, based on free software" was revised. The objective of the team leader was to give me the opportunity to have, by the end of my stay, a good grasp of all the ICTs activities at the DISD. However, I was more involved in outreach and partnership activities. Some of the work required traveling out of Ethiopia and took me to Port Louis in Mauritius, Grahams town in South Africa and Bamako in Mali.

Difficulties Encountered

One of the difficulties I encountered during my stay was the overwhelming number of acronyms I had to deal with at the DISD. They constituted an important part of the vocabulary used in daily activities and I needed to understand their meaning as quickly as possible. As a matter of fact, there was almost no induction period at the DISD. "You had to start running as soon as you hit the ground." In addition to the acronyms, I was the first United Nations Fulbright Fellow at ECA, and there was not any previous in-house experience I could benefit from.

Positive Outcomes

My internship at the DISD was very informative. My deep involvement in the activities of the ICTs team as well as attending international seminars, conferences and symposia on ICTs-related topics, made me gain valuable substantial knowledge.

I learned a lot about:

- The overall state of ICTs in Africa and the effort made by ECA and other partners to promote the use of these technologies for the development of the continent;
- The critical importance of policies and strategies in the use of Information and Communication Technologies for Development, and particularly in developing countries;
- The high need for African countries to engage in solid multi-stakeholder partnership and networking in Information and Communication Technologies for Development initiatives;
- E-government including the concept (G2G, G2B and G2C), the model (publish, interact, transact), the benefits (transparency, accountability, participatory, leapfrog etc..), the risks (illiteracy), the challenges (infrastructure, political will, skills etc..), and some showcases in Africa;
- Open source software as a cost effective alternative to proprietary software for African countries.

I also met and interacted with a good number of people at various DISD events (conferences, seminars, symposiums, forums, meetings, workshop, etc.), and made many new friends.

A Plea

Many development agencies and donors are currently involved in information and communication technologies initiatives for the development of Africa. However, there is room for more, especially in the area of Research and Development. My plea to the United Nations Foundation/Better World Fund would be to consider extending its current areas of activities (children's health; environment; peace, security and human rights; women and population) to specifically include information and communication technologies for the development of developing countries.

Acknowledgment

I would like to express my gratitude to:

The United Nations Foundation/Better World Fund and the Institute of International Education for the opportunity given to me to acquire working experience at the United Nations;

The ECA/DISD staff and especially Ms Aida Opoku-Mensah, the ICTs team leader, for their good guidance during my internship;

Prof. Maurice Tchuente, Cameroon Minister of Higher Education and Prof. Jean Louis Dongmo, Rector of Dschang University for authorizing an extension of my Fulbright training period to accommodate the internship;

The UN Fulbright Fellowship program management team, especially Susan Meyers, Jan Beagle, Caroline Vaughan, Mary E. Kirk, Carol E. Tegen and Kari A. Kuja for their assistance during the orientation and the wrap-up sessions;

Conclusion

The United Nations Fulbright Fellowship opportunity given to me to cap off my Masters program in Information Systems was very timely and valuable. Given my interests in Information and Communication Technologies for Development, the Economic Commission for Africa, coordinator of the African Information Society Initiative could not be a more appropriate place.

The six-month period at ECA was very rewarding. It provided me with greater understanding of Information and Communication Technologies for Development. At the end of my internship, I was more than ever before comforted in my belief that these technologies could effectively help to leapfrog the development in Africa. The conditions would be long-term vision, political will, and solid and sustained multi stakeholder partnerships. My internship at ECA also gave me the opportunity to contribute to the activities of the Development Information Service Division. I hope that the few suggestions made from my candid observations of these activities would contribute to the achievement of the AISI goal.

I wish that the United Nations Foundation/Better World Fund and the Institute of International Education would take necessary measures to sustain the United Nation Fulbright Fellowship program in order to give to many more Fulbrighters the opportunity to learn from UN professionals and to contribute to build a better world.

ngamassi@yahoo.fr

A Fulbright Experience of Love, Self-understanding and Self-emancipation

Lynette J. Chua - Malaysia

When I first sat down to write this essay, I failed. I tried to write about differences between me and my American friends, and my home country and the U.S., but the tone of the essay bothered me. Then it hit me. This essay was personal. I had to write about something that mattered deeply to me, and writing about differences between "us" and "them" did not flow from my heart. My circumstances are different from many Fulbrighters. I am a first-time Fulbright scholar but also a second-time student in the U.S. This current American experience, as a Fulbrighter, is built upon my previous experience as an undergraduate. I asked myself how the two experiences connected to each other, and how together they have changed my life. I mined my emotions and struck those that had gnawed at my heart since I left Malaysia to study in the U.S. for the first time. To express them, I realized I had to write about similarities instead.

So this essay is not about differences. Nor is it about culture shock. It is about similarities – about finding similarities, understanding them to be similarities and securing freedom from that revelation.

It is the only type of essay I can write about my experience as a Fulbrighter in the U.S. I have never felt as though I am experiencing the U.S. as an outsider or someone from a different culture, for I have always felt at home here. Hence, this is an essay about why I feel fundamentally similar to my American friends, how that feeling affected my relationship with my parents, and how the Fulbright experience gave me the opportunity – a second chance – to understand why our relationship was affected, to free myself from the agony of not understanding why our relationship was affected, and to liberate myself by knowing I can still love my parents after all these years.

I arrived in California in August 2005 to begin my journey as a Malaysian Fulbrighter and Ph.D. student in Berkeley's Jurisprudence and Social Policy program. I was the only student of my cohort to have come from halfway around the world. My partner, Anthony, sacrificed his career to relocate with me. He knew how much this opportunity meant to me. So did the loved ones of my classmates, who came from around the U.S. They, too, knew how much this opportunity at Berkeley meant to my classmates. They, too, gave up their familiar lives and relocated to Berkeley with my classmates. My classmates, their families, Anthony and I shared a similarity called love.

But to talk about love and my Fulbright experience, I must first go back ten years in time, when I came to the U.S. for my undergraduate studies at the E.W. Scripps School of Journalism, Ohio University. It was my first time away from home, and I could not wait. For 12 years, my parents had insisted that I receive an education in the Chinese language. So I did – six years of primary (grade) school in a public system and six years of secondary (high) school education in a private system set up by Chinese Malaysians. I loved and resented those 12 years. I loved them, because of friends and teachers, and the love and friendship built and preserved to this day. I resented them, because of the reason I was in Chinese-language schools. My parents believed that a Chinese education was academically and, most importantly (but most appalling to me), morally superior to any other form of education. I revolted at such irrationality, ignorance and ethnocentrism. Yes, I enjoyed school. I learned something, but how could my education possibly be the most superior? Based on the biased judgment of two human beings who had never lived or studied anywhere else in their lives? I completed those 12 years of education, initially with indifference to my parents' rationale (or lack thereof), and increasingly with disappointment at their prejudices as I developed a mind of my own. A latent rift between me and parents began to ferment, to surface after my first American experience. Perhaps to some people, I excelled in my studies, but I abhorred, refused and rejected my parents' rationale for studying in those schools.

Yet, life was ironic for my parents. They also wanted me to have what they considered to be a successful future. For that, they turned to the mastery of the English language.[14] From age four, I learned English from British language teachers and then at special English-learning centers. I read more English books in my 15 years of English-learning than Chinese books in my 12 years of formal Chinese education. Ideas came more easily when I thought in English rather than in Chinese. I expressed myself better in English. My English language ability was indeed an important key to my future, though not one contemplated and planned by my parents. It was the key to my independence from their stifling and bigoted worldview.

After graduating from high school, I submitted college applications to the other side of the world, the U.S. My parents wanted me to study somewhere closer. Maybe Australia? No way. I was not about to settle for 7 hours of flight time, when I knew 18 hours existed. This was my opportunity, and I wrestled it from them, ripped it from their clutches, as I boarded the plane, on my way to Athens, Ohio, U.S.A., where I began my first American journey as a journalism student and, subsequently, a journalist.

---

[14] English was taught as a second language in my Chinese schools. Few students achieve a high level of fluency.

I chose journalism, because I had never experienced an environment of free speech and free press in Malaysia. To my parents, challenging the government was foolhardy. They believed in the unquestioning pursuit of economic success, of which they had high expectations that I would undoubtedly achieve. Journalism became my gateway to freedom from the life expected of me. I wanted to see the world. I wanted to learn about other lives, other cultures and other ideas. All of those I tasted, as a journalism student – tided through the 1997 Asian economic crisis with generous U.S.-based scholarships and interest-free loans – and as a journalist in Nashville, Tennessee, the capital of country music.

After I returned, my parents thought I had changed. My parents have always preached that "we" were different from Americans, because "we" care about our families; "they" didn't. Translation: "we," like their bias for Chinese education, were morally superior. After my return, I became defensive. Whenever my parents accused Americans, or Westerners – their erroneous monolithic categorization – of not caring about their families or being cold, I would get furious. Their arrogance incensed me. Most of all, their ignorance infuriated me. They talked about millions of people from culturally diverse backgrounds and of different social classes as a monolithic group and denigrated them when they have not known a single American in their entire lives. Many casual conversations with my parents often spiraled down into "I have become Americanized" diatribes, because I no longer saw the world the way they expected me to – their way. Back then, I could not understand why my parents thought I had changed. For the past 10 years, I lived with the pain that my parents misunderstood me, my inability to identify that misunderstanding, and my failure to articulate that hurt.

I had given up hope of ever freeing myself from that pain. Then Fulbright sent me on my second American journey. Redemption became possible. I realized I had not changed since my first experience in the U.S. Love and family are still important to me, while my parents thought they were not, simply because I had discovered and believed that love and the importance of family transcended boundaries, including American borders, and that they transcend superficial differences between "us" and "them." My second Fulbright experience crystallized what I had found on my first journey but was unable to realize and articulate.

During my first experience in the U.S., as an undergraduate at Ohio University, I witnessed my American roommates' parents descend on them over the weekends, fuss over their diets and scrutinize their new friends anxiously. At that time, I was only glad a distance of half a globe apart saved me from the same regular embarrassment, but I knew my parents would have done the same, because they – like the parents of my American roommates – love their child. I saw my American friends rush hundreds of miles home, because they were needed suddenly. They went home, because family mattered to them. When my grandmother died while I was taking my final exams in 1998, I wished I could also jump into a car, step on the gas and pull into the driveway I had known for 18 years. During those times, my heart would ache, because family mattered to me, too, as it did to my American friends.

After graduation, I moved to Nashville, Tennessee, to work as a full-time newspaper reporter. I covered local politics and communities. The stories I wrote often touched on love and family. Education news told of parents' concern for their children; success stories of small businesses reflected family support for the entrepreneurs; so-called human interest stories more often than not evolved around humanity, heroism and love. At my workplace, I also noticed the pictures of parents, siblings, partners and children on cubicle walls, desks and workstations of my American colleagues. I added mine to the hodge-podge collection in the newsroom. These were little expressions of love. My American colleagues often invited me to their homes, and there I saw the same warmth, love and occasional squabbles that I find in my own family.

Perhaps ten years ago, I was less mature, and could not articulate why I did not find "us" fundamentally different from "them." The answer, which I have now discovered, is that "we" share an important similarity with "them," and the similarity is love. Back then, I did not realize that it was this similarity that bonded "us" with "them," not distinguished one from the other. This similarity was the root cause of my anger and frustration with my parents when they speak unfavorably of Americans and their country, and accused me of accepting the "decadent West." But ten years ago, I could not identify the root cause, and the failure to do so revealed the latent rift between me and my parents.

Discovering the root cause of our rift and healing that pain surprisingly became possible in my second American experience that Fulbright materialized for me. After working in Nashville, Tennessee, for 14 months, I decided to return to Southeast Asia. I thought being closer to family might help to mend the relationship. It did not. I studied law at the National University of Singapore, and later worked as a media policy officer for the Singapore government. The more capable I became of critical thinking, and the more exposed I was to government rhetoric about the East versus the West, the more I disagreed with my parents, and the deeper the rift ran. While in Singapore, I met and married Anthony, who not only loves me but also, unlike my parents, truly understands me. When I decided I wanted to pursue my studies further, he threw his support behind me, and "came along for the ride," as he called it. Because I was interested in law and its relationship with government and society, I applied to Berkeley's Jurisprudence and Social Policy doctoral program. Fulbright became an obvious funding opportunity. Academically, it all worked out. Berkeley accepted me; Fulbright welcomed me. However, I braced for the worst with my parents. My first American experience surfaced the latent rift that existed between me and my parents when I was a teenager, quietly resisting their ethnocentric brainwashing that my education and "culture" were morally superior. I expected my second American journey to exacerbate it.

So I arrived in Berkeley, full of hope for my academic future and with none for my relationship with my parents. I surprised myself. The surprise did not come from school – I settled happily into life as a Ph.D. student. Nor did the surprise bear out of living in the U.S. – it was no culture shock to me. I enthusiastically made it home again. In fact, in some ways, returning to the U.S. seemed like "coming home" as I reunited with old friends and visited my alma mater in Ohio. Instead, the surprise sprang from discovering that healing the pain caused by the rift between me and my parents was possible after all. The possibility emerged as I once again saw love in my American friends' life. However, unlike ten years ago, this time I did realize that it was love that made "us" and "them" fundamentally similar, and therefore, differentiated my views from my parents'. I saw fundamental similarity in our humanity; they could not. I can never and do not expect to change my parents' thinking, but knowing the root cause of our rift healed the pain for me.

To study at Berkeley, one of my classmates moved from the other side of the U.S. Her partner* and children came along, uprooting his career and their children's social network. He had to find a new job. They had to fit into new schools, try to make new friends, and get used to mommy's new schedule. Another classmate and her partner also relocated from the other side of the country. He requested for a job transfer. With him came their books, wedding photos and family albums. Two classmates' partners quit their jobs to come here, not knowing where their next paychecks will come from. Yet another classmate's partner packed her bags and plunged into beginning a new life as a student on the same campus. They all came, because they cared about their families, and because they loved one another.

Anthony could have continued his career back in Southeast Asia. He could have asked me to stay behind. He could have told me to come here on my own. But he could not bear the thought of being separated from me. He could not bear risking our future as a family. Without any inkling of his prospects here, he, too, packed

---

* I use the gender-neutral term of "partner," because love not only transcends customs and national boundaries, but it also transcends gender.

his bags and plunged himself into the unknown. He chose what he considered to be the only option, simply because he loved me.

Anthony and I moved from halfway around the world. My classmates and their loved ones only moved from other parts of the U.S. However, the difference is that of physical distance. This difference in miles is extinguished by the same unquantifiable nature of love. My classmates and I share the same unknown – we do not know what the future will hold for us after we finally complete, bind and file our dissertations maybe in five or six years time. Our paths will probably diverge afterward. But we take comfort in one thing we have in common – support from our loved ones, who will always be there to support us.

Within five months, on my second American journey and as a Fulbrighter, I have freed myself from the agony of ten years. I understand it now. My parents still misunderstand me. But now I understand why. I find similarities where they see differences, and I defend that discovery – that people, regardless of nationalities and cultures, are bound together by love, are moved by love enough to make sacrifices.

Thus, my Fulbright experience is not about crossing customs. Rather, it is about an opportunity – a second chance – to cross barriers to self-understanding and self-emancipation. My parents will never comprehend why they misunderstand me. But I do not blame them. They had given me the opportunity – the opportunity they never had – the first time around to discover another world, even as I yanked it painfully from them, because they love me. I did discover a new world – one with similarities to the one of my origins. Without that first opportunity, I would not have had this second one. So I forgive my parents for misunderstanding, because they did not know any better, and simply because I love them too. Without this second opportunity, made possible by Fulbright, I would not have crossed into self-understanding and self-emancipation; and, without Anthony, I would not have realized that it was the similarity of having love that I shared with my American classmates. Thus, this essay is for my parents, who began all of this, for Fulbright, who believed, and for Anthony, who made my writing it possible.

lynette.chua@gmail.com

Get back to where you now belong

Katja Ziehmayer - Austria

I was 29 when I moved to America and had always considered myself a European through and through. Of course I had been to the US before, and even made some very good friends there; when I finally arrived, they expected me with open arms – and in my friend Howard's case, on top of that, with a bag of bagels.

I had applied for a Fulbright scholarship because there were hardly any job prospects back home with a degree in History and English, and I was hoping that the skills I would acquire at my MA program of Industrial and Organizational Psychology would provide me with better opportunities once I returned to Europe. I would definitely return as I had no aspirations to spend the rest of my life in the United States, unlike some of my friends in Vienna.

It all began when I made an appointment with Steve, the Human Resource Director of Coca-Cola Central Europe, Eurasia and Northern Africa, where I was working at the time. This office was the acting headquarter for 52 countries, which obviously meant that HR had a lot of employees to keep happy. Steve held a crucial position, and by talking to him I hoped to gain some insight into the field of HR - which had always interested me. It may sound trite, but when I parked my car that morning I had the distinct feeling that the meeting with Steve would change my life. I walked into his office and asked him outright what it would take to (one day) get his job. Steve suggested that I should not follow the standard route for getting a degree in Human Resource Management, but try I/O Psychology, which is geared towards improving satisfaction and productivity of people at work by applying psychological principles and methods. "I know you, Katja" Steve said. "You like people, and you'll like this." And to show me how much he was convinced that I would succeed in this program, Steve also wrote me a reference letter for my Fulbright application.

Naturally I was elated when I was accepted by the Fulbright Commission, but there was also a grain of doubt: did I really want to spend such a long time away from my friends and family? I had always been of the impression that some people were fleeing something if they left their home. I was leading a very comfortable life in Vienna. Apart from the dire job prospects as a historian, I had no reason to try my luck elsewhere. In the end I put all my worries aside and just started to look forward to what was to come.

I hardly suffered from any sort of culture shock when I settled in at my new life in New Haven, Connecticut. I adapted to my new surroundings and circumstances quite easily. At heart I still felt that Europe, in particular Vienna was my home, and that was the place I would gladly return to after my program was over. So it was no surprise that during my first one and a half years I enjoyed being the foreigner, holding up my homeland's traditions by voting for a new president by absentee ballot, commemorating all the important Austrian holidays by calling my family, and adding my own two (Euro) cents in discussions at my university by interjecting, "In Europe, we always…". I was content being somewhat of an outsider, because I knew that there was a place that I truly belonged to.

Finishing up my studies had been more cumbersome than I had imagined. Also, I had hit a rough spot with my roommate, which had forced me to move out of our apartment in February. I was extremely fortunate that my boyfriend's parents, who lived in a neighboring town, were kind enough to take me in on a short notice. Eric, my boyfriend, was attending graduate school in Knoxville at that time, and we had made plans to move in together once my program was over. My last classes were getting stressful and I was longing to graduate.

On top of my course load I was working three jobs at the time: one much hated research assistantship at school, a great teaching assistantship, also at school, and a job at a small HR consulting firm. I loved this last position, I adored and respected my boss, but I thought that I had worked really hard over the past months. It was time to take a break.

In early March I got an unexpected phone call from my best friend Annette. While I was away studying in the US she had moved to Barcelona and was living there with her boyfriend Alberto. I had not seen her in 1 ½ years, and because of unfortunate circumstances she hadn't been able to attend my Farewell Party in Vienna in early September of 2003. I missed her, and was of the opinion that we didn't stay in touch as much as I might have liked. When she called I was immediately reminded of how much I wanted to see her again, and when she told me that she definitely had enough room to put me up, and would love to see me, too, I made up my mind at the spur of the moment and agreed to visit.

Eric didn't seem too surprised when I filled him in on my plans. "She's your best friend! I know you haven't seen her in so long, and you definitely deserve a little vacation after all the stress of the last two months. Once you've moved to Tennessee with your cat and found a job you'll hardly have time to travel anyway. It'll do you good to get out a little bit."

I was weighing my options and the thought of strolling around Barcelona, in the spring sunshine and in the company of someone who means a lot to me, sounded more and more tempting. I talked to my boss at the consulting firm (the assistantship at school would be over by then) and I asked Eric's parents if they would be able to take care of my cat, and in due time booked a flight to Spain and a seat on the shuttle to Newark Airport. I could hardly idle away the hours until the last day of my program, as if I was a teenager again in high school, anxiously awaiting summer break. I had only been to Vienna once during my studies, and the mere thought of being among "my people" again hardly let me sit still during the 8 hour flight to Paris.

Since I had had class that Thursday, I could only leave on Friday night, which would bring me to Europe early Saturday morning (or so I thought). My plan had been to meet up with my other best friend Verena at the Barcelona airport. She had just been visiting Annette for a few days with her boyfriend and although it hadn't been possible for me to be there in time to spend more than a few hours with them, we had arranged to have a reunion at one of the airport's cafes.

The first omen that things were not exactly going as I would have liked materialized when – even though my plane out of Newark had not been delayed – me and a few others were not allowed to board the connecting flight in Paris/Charles de Gaulle. The airport crew had closed the doors well before the actual departure time, and we had to spend more than 20 excruciating minutes watching the plane sit at the gate – right in front of our noses – with its doors closed, while several of the less tired passengers of my flight tried to argue with the airport personnel not to let us miss our connecting flight. Surely we had not been late. They must have known at the gate that we were coming, and after all, the plane was still there! Couldn't they make an exception and open the doors again?

Maybe they could have, but they didn't. The plane left without me. I was stuck at the Paris airport for a few hours, unable to get in touch with Annette. For some reason my cell phone – although tri-band - did not work, and the phone cards that Air France had given us were no good, either. I placed a call on my credit card, to let my friends in Spain know that I would be delayed for several hours and therefore miss our brunch date with Verena. In addition, I hardly had any euros with me, so I sat hungry and tired at the gate, waiting to continue on to my destination.

When I finally got to Barcelona, Annette was waving an enormous bunch of flowers in the air, which she gave to me in honor of my upcoming graduation. I was thrilled to be back in a city, and climbed on the bus going to town with an expression of total rapture on my face, which had Annette and Alberto in tears of laughter. The first night was spent talking, simply catching up, and enjoying each other's company.

Since I didn't have a lot of time for sightseeing I was thankful that Annette volunteered to take me around the city on Sunday. I was still a little bummed out that my cell phone did not work because that meant that talking to Eric would be a little bit of a problem. Alberto had given me a spare phone they had at the house so that I would not have to use a pay phone all the time. This was also means for my two friends to reach me during the few days I was visiting.

After a day of strolling around Barcelona, meeting some of Annette's Spanish friends and making pictures, Annette and I wanted to meet Alberto and his friend for dinner. Unfortunately, the table at the restaurant we had chosen was not available, so we decided to wait in a bar across the street. We ordered drinks and sat in a circle on high bar stools, chatting away, agitated. After half an hour we left and went back to the restaurant, but to no avail – there was still no table for us. So back we went into the little bar, and took possession of the bar stools again.

Another half hour later we were getting really hungry and got up again to try our luck at the restaurant for a third time. We were laughing, joking, and generally having a good time when we got up from our barstools, but a second later it hit me like lighting: I couldn't find my purse. It had been under my chair, but it was gone.

I had never lost anything that important before, and at first, I was sure that the purse was probably just hidden under somebody else's chair, or that I had inadvertently pushed it to the side. I told Annette that my purse was missing, and we started looking for it together. It was nowhere to be found. Somebody must have stolen it!

To this day it is a mystery to me how anybody could have fished out my relatively large tote bag from where it was sitting under my chair, propped against a wall. We had all been sitting in a close circle, and whoever did it must have come up close behind me, bent down, and then reached around the legs of the barstool to get to it – hardly a maneuver that one might think goes by unnoticed.

After a few moments of frantic searching it dawned on me: my wallet! My camera! The postcards I had bought! And most important of all: my passport!

We left the bar after we had asked everybody around us, including the waiter, if they had seen anything. They hadn't. Outside on the street I was thankful for the brisk air of a spring evening. For the first few minutes I was hopeful that the thief had thrown the purse, after taking the cash and immediate valuables like my camera, into a trash can. We split up into two groups, searching the neighborhood in order to achieve what soon dawned on me as a futile effort. Whoever had taken my purse had taken it to a place where I could not go. The trash cans were full of discarded items; one even contained an old suitcase, but nothing that even remotely resembled my grey bag.

My evening was ruined, and I wanted to go home. Annette did her best to cheer me up, promising that we would try the city's Lost & Found the next day, but in the end the only thing that remained for her to do was to watch me grow more and more desperate. On our way to her apartment I was going through the list of items that had been in my bag, and what it would cost me – quite literally, and also in terms of effort – to replace them. I knew my own cell phone was safe in my suitcase, and I had a couple of dollars stashed away in my other jacket. Being the organized person that I am, I had even brought copies of my passport and visa, as I always did when I was going on an international trip. I knew I had someone to rely on for help, and assistance in battling the authorities. My Spanish was far from perfect, and I was dreading the next day, to talk to the appropriate authorities and take care of things, so that I could eventually get back to the States.

Still, my furthermost problem was that I had no idea how I would achieve exactly that. I could live without my glasses for the moment, but without a passport and a valid visa there was no way that I would be granted entry by US immigration. Would I have to go home to Austria? Would I not be able to graduate, because I missed the deadline for the one final report I still had to write? What would happen to my belongings, above all my beloved cat? I was tossing and turning in bed that night, trying to figure out all the necessary steps to get back to New Haven within the shortest amount of time. After a while, I realized it was hopeless, so I got up and opened my laptop. The US embassy was in Madrid, and there was only an American consulate in Barcelona, which I knew was not supposed to issue visas. But what if it was an emergency, like mine? Clearly somebody would be able to help me. After two hours of scanning the internet for valuable information, and almost four pages of notes, I went to bed.

The next day was a Monday, and I set out early. My first trip led me to the Austrian consulate, where a young woman was very sympathetic to my misery, and promised to help. She commended me on my good sense in making copies of my documents. Before she could issue me a temporary passport, she needed me to officially report my old one stolen, and have some pictures taken. Coincidentally, a little photograph store was located in the same building as the Austrian consulate. Since I knew that the American visa required a different size than the Austrian passport picture, I got two sets. I looked positively scraggly, with my pigtails askew and a crooked smile on my face because the photographer was trying to make me laugh. My rudimentary Spanish seemed to have been sufficient to convey that I was clearly a "damsel in distress", and didn't have much to smile about these days. Finally, I was able to pay for the pictures with the last few Euros from my pocket. I would have to ask Annette to exchange my dollars later.

At the police station, I stood in line for over an hour, until I was told at the counter that this had definitely been the wrong line to wait in. In the second line I met a nice Scotsman, who, during our comparably short wait, was constantly chided for his foolishness by his Spanish girlfriend, "Who puts his wallet, with all the IDs he's ever had, in his jacket pocket and then hangs this jacket over a chair in a club? Es stupido! This was practically an invitation to have it stolen!" Listening in on their discussion, I felt like I was being yelled at, too, for not having taken more precautions against any thieves.

It was a long ordeal, and I will spare you, honored reader, of more lurid details. At the end of that day, I held my new, albeit temporary, Austrian passport in my hands. My credit cards were canceled, and a cash advance from my bank in Connecticut on the way via Western Union. I had printed and filled out all the necessary forms for a new visa, and made an appointment at the embassy in Madrid. The consulate in Barcelona had not been able to help me, so Alberto booked me a flight to the Spanish capital for early Wednesday morning, the day I was actually supposed to return to the US. There was nothing more I could do, but hope for the best.

On Wednesday, I was nervous but fairly confident that everything would go according to plan. There would be more than ample time to get everything resolved in Madrid because my return flight to Barcelona was not before 9 o'clock that same night. I got to the embassy with half an hour to spare, and almost happily stood in line, knowing my grievances were soon going to be over. But once again fate seemed to have something else in mind: the guard at the door of the embassy told me bluntly that I would not be allowed inside with the small backpack I was carrying. "No backpacks", he said, pointing to a big sign that said exactly that in English and Spanish.

I crumbled at this turn of events at a time when I had almost seen the sun rising on the horizon. "What am I supposed to do? I have an appointment at 10:30, and I don't know anybody in the city! Where do you think I should leave my bag? I need my visa! I just want to go home!" None of my pleading could persuade the guard otherwise, he just kept pointing to the sign. "You have till 12:30. That's when we close for the public. If you're not here by then, you'll have to come back tomorrow."

As I turned away from the gate, crying, I felt as if once again something was being taken from me. It wasn't that I was particularly partial to my backpack, but I could not stomach the thought of giving it up; surrendering by dropping it into a trash can simply felt wrong. My bag contained the documents I would need at the embassy, some food, a book and a small plush cow I had bought at the airport for my boyfriend. If you squeezed it, it mooed. It gave me consolation, and I didn't want to throw it away just like that.

Within minutes I was running down the street, asking at stores if they would let me drop off my backpack there. Somebody at a Starbucks told me about a department store a few blocks away which used to have lockers. It turned out that due to the increase in terrorism the store had decided to get rid of the lockers, and it was hard for me to be angry at the salespeople who turned me away. I was crying, stammering in pidgin Spanish, blubbering a request that might possibly turn out to be dangerous. After half an hour I realized the futility of my efforts, and instead developed a new plan. I would go to the nearest police office, and ask them for help. It was only a bag! Wasn't the most important thing that I would get my visa and be able to get home?

The police men were more than sympathetic. Clearly, judging by the toilet paper rolls in the waiting area, bawling foreigners were a well-known sight at the police station. After we had established that I did not want to file a report that something had been stolen, but actually leave my things in their custody, an officer searched the bag. He happened to squeeze my plush cow, and it mooed. It seems to be fair to say that mine was clearly one of the more ridiculous requests he had to deal with that day.

At 11:45am I was back on my way. In my fervor to bring my bag to the police station I had forgotten how far I had been walking; now my feet were blistered and bloody and I took the subway for the two stops to the embassy. This time, there were no problems at the gate. As I sat inside, waiting for my turn, only one thought was on my mind: I'm going to be home soon, as in New Haven, Connecticut.

Usually the embassy sends the passport back to the visa applicant, which can take up to a week, but exceptions can be made. Still, the officer who attended to me was doubtful that the consular would have time to sign my visa that same day. He couldn't promise me anything, and was not moved by my pleadings. Without my passport, the only means of identification at the time, I could not fly back to Barcelona. Where would I stay that night? All of my money and credit cards had been stolen as well, and the cash advance from my bank in the US was already dwindling because Air France would not let me change my return ticket, but instead forced me to buy a new one. I was told to wait until 5:00pm, and if I was lucky I would get my visa then.

The rest of the afternoon went by in a haze. I sat at the very same Starbucks that had earlier turned me down when I wanted them to let me drop off my backpack. Stripped of anything to read, I wrote lengthy lamentations about my misery in the little notebook I had kept with me. My knees were shaking when I made my way back across the street, and waited at the gate of the embassy. The guard who had formerly sent me away simply opened a small hatch in the bulletproof window he was lounging behind and handed me my passport. My brand new visa was signed, stamped and ready to accompany me home.

I have not left the United States ever since I came back from Spain that April. These days, I watch my purse like a hawk wherever I go, and I seem to have stopped bringing up the fact that I was not born in this country in every conversation. In May I will be returning to Vienna, and even though I'm really looking forward to being with my friends and family again, I know I will miss the States. Things have changed, and my perception of what is "home" has been expanded to people, places and objects I had previously never considered to have any special meaning to me. But isn't this exactly what I came here for, to expand my horizon?

Last October, Eric sent in his application to the US Fulbright program – he is planning to come to Austria with me. Watching me for almost two years now in my "new home" he became interested in trying his luck abroad too; he wants to leave what is familiar and move to a place that is "not yet home". And if he ever happens to go on a spontaneous trip to Spain, I'll make sure he tapes his passport to his ankle.

kcziehmayer@yahoo.com

My Second Life

Anouk Bachman - Netherlands

"Smeck, smeck, smeck, smeck". I couldn't stop staring at her big mouth decorated with cherry-red lipstick that had left little stains on her white teeth. It was beautiful and scary at the same time, a typical metaphor for Freud's *vagina dentata*. She was working on her chewing gum louder than I had ever heard anybody chew. "Smeck, smeck, smeck" it sounded, and I imagined that she would never do anything else but chew on that chewing gum of hers, just like a big and bored-looking version of that little girl from Charlie and the Chocolate Factory (the book, that is). It was not disgust that I felt, but an utter, jet-lag inflicted fascination for this woman that was the first person I met in a country that is still too big for my imagination.

You can drive from the North to the South of Holland in approximately five hours and it will take you maybe three hours to drive from the West side to the East side of the country. From my parents' house in the 600-year old city of Breda, it is only a four hour drive through the country of Belgium to the magnificent capital of France. If you know the uncanny feeling that you get when you really, deeply ponder the infinity of the universe, you know the feeling I got when I thought about the size of America and how far away it was from everything I knew. I always thought that when I moved from Breda to Amsterdam, which is a one hour drive by car, it would be as far away as I could stand to be from my family. I guess I was ready to test the flexibility of my own limits.

"How are ya'?", she asked me, while I could see the pink gum clenched between her jaws. "I am okay", I replied, "I have had a fairly good flight, but the food was horrible. But then I shouldn't complain since…". I stopped talking because the woman had abruptly stopped her chewing and was staring at me as if I was telling her my entire life-story. She looked bored and annoyed. Clearly I was never supposed to give an answer to her question. I already thought it was awkward for an employee at customs to express such an interest in my well-being. She resumed her chewing and shouted "Next!" before I had even packed my papers again.

I proceeded through the hall of Philadelphia airport, where I had to wait for five hours for my connecting flight to San Francisco. This was it; my first official gateway to my new life in America and who knew what could come after that. It wasn't as cool as I thought it would be though. The terminal gave me the creepy feeling of being a character in an episode of the 60's TV-series The Twilight Zone. I was this girl trapped in a weird empty zone between her two lives, which she has to maintain at the same time. To do that, she must travel to and from her different lives and pass through the Twilight Zone, a constant changing; never lasting area where nobody resides and everybody is in a hurry. One day she gets trapped in the zone because she missed her flight, and she cries out for help to other travelers, but they don't respond since the zone is just a temporary phase and they too, don't want to stay there.

My empty stomach warned me to stop daydreaming, for the food that I was served in the airplane wasn't accepted by my bowels and by now, I was starving. The many airports that I had visited before in my life, like the ones in Amsterdam, Rome, Melbourne and Kuala Lumpur, had always had some kind of cafeteria with decent food. Philadelphia airport offered me more choice in take-outs than I had ever seen in one place, but none looked very appealing. The people seemed to be shouting at each other and their sneering accents felt like a beaver was gnawing at my tired brains. I decided to have a fairly decent looking French baguette with ham, cheese and some vegetables. The girl at the counter looked a little bit like the woman at customs, although she was not nearly as interesting because she lacked the gum. She also asked me how I was. This time I answered by giving her just a smile and returning the question, to which she never answered. That was too bad, since I really did wonder what it was like to work in a place where your customers come from all over the world, with different cultures, languages and stories. Maybe I was too romantic, but her job seemed to be more interesting than any of my previous jobs. I remember working at an Italian ice cream salon for a summer, and gaining ten kg in a very short time as it was my job, next to serving, to taste the new ice cream flavors before they would be sold. The old Italian man who made the ice cream was a master at his work and he came up with waffle-flavored, apple pie-flavored, licorice-flavored and even the surprisingly well tasting spinach-flavored ice cream. I made sure the licorice ice cream never made it to the salon.

I noticed that I must have been ripped off by paying eight dollars for that baguette which, by the way, tasted exactly like rubber. Also the ocean of Starbucks coffee made me feel sick and I had to make a run for the bathroom. As if faith had wanted to drag me into the malpractice of stereotyping, I witnessed two people on my way to the restrooms, who just happened to be so fat that they had to be put on a little cart and driven to their gate, because their weight was just too much for their legs to carry. It was a couple with cowboy hats on their heads and the woman was chewing on something I couldn't identify. I decided that for the time being that I really, really, disliked America and everything in it.

Luckily that was more my homesickness and fiery character thinking. As soon as my plane circled over the city by the Bay, my final destination, I felt that exciting travel-buzz again. I felt like a cool, tough, real woman-of-the-world who is making it on her own, a strong girl from the tiny country of the Netherlands who is going to make it in the world of academics. I felt like the star in the world's movie, until I finally fell in my boyfriend's arms and started sobbing uncontrollably. Already I missed my family and friends so much that I wouldn't mind taking the same 18-hour trip right back! Poor Alex picked up an emotional wreck from the airport that day, and for weeks I was walking around in the city as if it were a dream of which I still wasn't sure whether I wanted to wake up or not. I moved in with Alex, who, at that point, had been my long-distance boyfriend for almost a year. We met at his promotional tour for a new video game he designed, and I was to interview him that day in Amsterdam. It was love at first sight, and for a long time we e-mailed, chatted, phoned and traveled around as much as possible. When he had a press tour in Paris, I drove down and picked him up to party with me in Amsterdam for one night. We even bought webcams, but that wasn't a big success since both of us didn't know how to use them. I was supposed to go to Sydney, Australia on an exchange program that winter, but I decided to put those plans aside and put all my efforts into being able to live with Alex in San Francisco. Of course it helped to find out that San Francisco would be the best place for my studies on video games anyway, and that for an academic career, nothing would be better for me than to study there. I worked hard and I was rewarded with a Fulbright Scholarship, which meant that my life would change drastically and that for at least the time that it would take me to finish my Master's, I would be living in the States. I was ecstatic! Finally being with Alex was great and although I felt homesick and I followed him around like a little puppy afraid of losing its way. I knew I would be fine in this country of opportunities.

Alex and I needed a slightly bigger apartment than the studio we shared and it was up to me to go house hunting. I ventured out on the streets and hills of San Francisco, breathing in the cool breeze from the ocean. It was great to get to know the city by myself, armed with a map and a bottle of water. The rent was shocking, and I found out that it is impossible to rent a decent one-bedroom apartment for less than 1200 dollars a month. I found a little studio-apartment for me and Alex on the top of the hill in the neighborhood the Haight, around the corner of the place where Janis Joplin used to live. It is the area where the hippies started their liberal ways of living in the 60's, the area where the band The Grateful Dead had their home base and the area where artists and singers performed on the streets. However, when Alex and I moved in, its streets were filled with homeless junkies begging for change and the famous corner of the streets Haight - Ashbury was dishonored with the fungus of the multinational GAP. Apart from the covered-up bullet holes in our apartment, it was a great and dynamic place to live.

After weeks of house hunting and roaming around in the city, university started and my own life in the US finally took off. It also meant that from then on I was actively participating in the American way of life, of which I could never have thought to be so different from my Dutch roots. It was a compilation of many little things and subtleties that caused a light culture shock. First of all there was the food. The amount of choices and options that one has in an American supermarket, but still the utter lack of reasonable products, almost drove me crazy. I struggled, especially to find dairy products that we are so fond of in the Netherlands. I tried to find normal, plain yoghurt, but from the dozens of different brands I could not pick any yoghurt that contained AND sugar, AND carbs, but not too much fat. Even an employee from the supermarket, a pale goofy teenager that reminded me of movie character Napoleon Dynamite, couldn't help me out. The choice was between either diet products or the whole full fat chocolate package. I decided to go for the sugar free yoghurt and bought a pack of sugar to add that to the white tasteless gob.

When you go out for dinner in America, it is normal that the server puts the bill on your table even before you have finished your meal. The first time this happened, it freaked me out. It must have been the most impolite behavior I have ever seen in a restaurant. I was so stunned that I didn't dare to ask the waitress why she did this. Instead, I vowed never to eat there again and left no tip. Of course, I eventually figured out that this is normal and happens all the time, but I still have a hard time getting over the feeling that they want you to finish your meal and get lost. Americans in general finish their meals quite fast, while in most European countries it's not uncommon to sit at a dinner table for three hours, having conversations and bottles of red wine. American restaurants are more economically orientated. You eat and drink, you pay, you leave and make place for the next customers.

Cultural differences make life exciting and my university life was about to take off, the sun was shining and my optimism knew no limits. My woman-of-the-world feeling returned when I found out how the public transport system in San Francisco worked, and especially when I walked on the university campus as if I had never done anything else. I rocked in the new and hip clothes that I had bought for my first day at university, just like I used to get a new dress every year at primary school. My classes were small; about fifteen people in each class, and the average age of my fellow graduate students in the humanities was high. There were some students of my age, around 24, 25, and others that had past their thirties a long time ago.

When the professor came in, I couldn't be more surprised. It was a dynamic woman in her forties with parts of her hair dyed in a bright red color. The other students immediately started commenting on how they loved her hair, and they asked the professor how her summer had been. Professor Bertram replied with an elaborate story about her adventures and while she was handing out the candy that she brought into her class, she took the time to listen to her students' discussions. Other professor may have had a more classical appearance, but all were very friendly and not one of them took on the "I am untouchable"-attitude of professors that I was used to. I loved it and I felt excited to dive into the heavy load of readings and assignments that we got.

Although I immediately loved the academic atmosphere at the San Francisco State University, which was so much less uptight and arrogant than the status-driven universities in the neighborhood, it still felt like an odd duck. I was older than the other foreign students, who were here on exchange programs instead of on a scholarship like me. This became painfully clear to me on a foreign students' night out. Dressed in sneakers, jeans and a plain shirt I joined the group of people from the foreign students club, and with many already having fake ID's, we entered a bar that would have been smoky if it was located anywhere in Europe. I sat down at the bar and ordered my regular double vodka without rocks and stared at the other girls who toke their sweaters off to reveal most of their beautiful bodies if it were not for a piece of cloth covering up their most interesting bits. The boys went wild, but four of the girls pushed them aside to climb on the big blocks that were placed around the dance floor. There they dance, or rather made coitus-like movements, sometimes grinding on each other's bodies and shouting something at the flock of boys that had gathered around their blocks. It reminded me of the many nature documentaries I had watched on the National Geographic Channel, in which the female or male birds would dance for their potential partners, showing off all the best feathers the had to offer before choosing a mate that was allowed to mount them.

Some of the boys tried to reach the girls by climbing on their blocks, but they were always dismissed, probably only till later in the night. I soon decided that I didn't want to join the foreign students club, since it seemed to me that their main focus was partying and although I love to go out and dance and drink, joining a club like that ruled out the possibility of meeting Americans with the same interests as me. That made it hard for me to make friends at first, since all the American students seemed to have established their groups a long time ago, and although they were all very open and friendly, an invitation from them to hang out was never followed by the actual practice of hanging out. It was another cultural difference that I found hard to deal with. Friendliness in America should not be confused with friendship. The warmth and openness of the American students that made me feel so welcome at first, led me to become disillusioned when I found out that invitations and very personal conversations should rarely be taken seriously. In the Netherlands people are, compared to in America, not very friendly, but very sincere. You will know for sure whether someone likes you or not and an invitation will go accompanied by the exchange of phone numbers to make sure that the promised 'hanging out' will happen. On the other hand, it did occur to me that the Dutch people may come across as 'cold' to American tourists and visitors and now I could better understand that, years ago, when I used to be a bartender at a club in Amsterdam, American tourists would tell not to be so rude or "shy".

Because I found it difficult to relate to other American students at first, I automatically found myself gravitating towards the two other Dutch students I met. They were here on an exchange program as they were of my age and were more serious about their studies in San Francisco than many other foreign students. We hung out together a lot, laughing about our clashes with American culture and how we missed silly things like cheese, European squares in cities, and a certain Dutch supermarket. Whenever I hung out with them I felt like being home again. It was funny that we all came from the same university in the same city in Holland, but that we had never met before and even if we did, we might not have felt the need to become friends in the familiar situation of home. Peer was a great and energetic guy. He mainly partied with a group of Italian students, but whenever he felt like a more serious or laid back conversation, he would turn to Christina and me. Christina and him developed a love-hate-relationship very soon. They were each other's opposites, with Christina being a strong-minded, liberal and politically conscious feminist and Peer an economically thinking, jolly student who didn't want to be too serious all the time. I loved listening to their heavy discussions, especially when I noticed that Peer took a great pleasure in teasing Christina by saying things that he knew would make her shout at him. When Peer left again, both me and Christina felt like there was a gap in our friendship.

One day I decided I needed to get to know more American students and I talked to a guy at university and told him that I was Dutch. "That's cool, I'm German too", he replied. I was confused and asked him something in German. "Oh, I don't speak German", he said, "but my great-grandparents were German, so I am German". "Well, that still doesn't make you Dutch", I smiled. He didn't understand. He thought that Dutch and German were the same, and later he let me know that the Netherlands were next to Sweden. I found it funny and I told him that would be really nice, since I love the cold winters that Sweden has. Normally I would think of him as ignorant and stupid, until I caught myself not being able to even name thirty of the American states. I guess that we just know mostly about the part of the world where we are from. I realized that the habit of many Europeans to blame Americans for their ignorance was unjust. Although there are exceptions, like the girl who thought that all Europeans speak the same language: "Euro".

Months went by and in time I felt more and more at ease with my new life in San Francisco. I slowly got to know some people from my classes and we even went out for drinks every week. I became friends with an American student called Jason, and when Thanksgiving was approaching, he invited me and Alex over to celebrate it at his parents' house. I eagerly accepted, since both Alex and I were not familiar with Thanksgiving and we were just dying to see how a real American family celebrates it. On Thanksgiving morning, Alex and I drove out to Jackson, a tiny town near the Sierra Nevada, in the middle of California.

Driving through the golden hills of the countryside, I looked at the trees and plants and I knew I had never seen such beautiful autumn colors before. We drove through several little towns that had the typical Western movies-feel to them. I saw pubs and shops with names like "The Golden Nugget", "The Golden Spade" and "Goldrush". These were all settlements that were built during the famous gold rush period in America, and it seemed as if nothing had changed ever since.

Jason drove out to meet us and he led us back to his parents' ranch. It was a classical Californian gold-rush ranch, with hundreds of acres of land surrounding it. We were greeted warmly by Jason's parents and his other family members. The Thanksgiving dinner that I had heard so much about, didn't last more than twenty minutes, after which we went out for a walk and a drink. Alex and I stayed over for the night in the family's trailer and the next morning I woke up early to the sound of people shouting. I quickly got dressed and stepped out in the pouring rain, where Jason's uncle greeted me and told me to put on some boots to help them chase the cows back into the barn. I could hardly believe that I was running around in the rain, chasing cows from the hills of the ranch to a barn that I thought I had seen before only in Westerns. If only my mother could have seen me then! We got the cows to the barn, where we had to count them and I heard that one little calf had to be castrated. Jason's uncle took out a scissor-like thing and he showed me how they would trap the animal and cut off its balls. However authentic the whole experience may have been, I did hide in the barn when it had to happen. Afterwards, Jason told me that the dust rags I thought I had seen were actually the webs of the infamous and lethal black widow spiders. I think I slept through the whole drive back to San Francisco, having dreams of giant spiders clipping off calf-balls with their jaws.

Back in San Francisco my work for my classes was piling up and I spent most of my days in front of my laptop at the university's cantina. One day I decided to give in to my hangover-induced desire for fat and I lined up at the hamburger place. There were two blonde cheerleader types standing in front of me and I remember admiring them for their beautiful bodies and toothpaste smiles. They were talking that typical cheerleader talk: "Oh Ashley, I gotta tell you. It's like, you know. Dan is just, like, well, he's so like. I just think he's awesome, you know?" What they were actually trying to say never made sense to me. They ordered the same ting as I did; a cheeseburger and fries. I sat down at my regular table in the corner and looked at the girls who joined their group of it-girls and jocks. I envied them and wished I belonged to a group of friends. Somehow I never really did. At the age of fourteen, when most girls start to blossom in their early womanhood, I fell behind. I was a quiet and shy girl who spent most of her time reading fantasy novels in her room and never had more than one or two friends which, in hindsight, should have been plenty. Silently I regarded the other girls as they walked down the school's halls in their beautiful clothes draped around their developing bodies. My body was still the same as it had always been to me. I had a round children's belly and my breasts were nowhere to be found. In agony I searched through the fashion magazines to look for the style that I should adapt to become popular. It was at that time that the whole western world fell for the "junkie-look" in top models. It was also at that time that I cut out all the ads that I could find with the model Kate Moss on it, and put them on my bedroom's walls. I wanted to be just like her.

That year, my grandfather whom I loved so dearly, died a gruesome death from lung cancer. The strongest and most beautiful man I had ever seen (my grandfather looked like Rober De Niro, but taller), shriveled away like a dying little bird. It was a long and agonizing process, and it made me question the fairness and purpose of life. My parents didn't raise me with any religion - although my father is Catholic - because they wanted me to be free to make my own choices in life. I wanted to believe in a God so bad, but never could and thus I grew up an atheist. Without that safety net of God's love, believing that what Karl Marx once said was true: Religion is opium for the people. My ontological questions couldn't be answered by anyone and I sunk into a deep adolescent depression. In an attempt to regain my confidence, I slowly started to eat less and less. I was fourteen years old and assumed that by looking like a model, I could become happy and popular. Next to that, I now think that I subconsciously also decided that I didn't want to grow up, that I wanted to stay in that unconcerned phase of life where decisions are made for you, and where appearances don't matter as long as your parents are there.

Soon my mother noticed my declining appetite and when she put me on a scale and saw that with my length of 1.70 meters I only weighed 45 kilos. She decided I needed help. I agreed, since I had known all the time that something was wrong with me, but I just couldn't grasp it. I went through a long process of treatments by different doctors and psychiatrists, but all they could do was to say that I was anorectic. Of course that was a conclusion I made myself a long time ago, but instead of looking into myself for help, I was hoping that others could help me regain the courage and will to live again. My doctors prescribed antidepressants for me, but it was of no use. At a weight of a mere 36 kilos the doctors decided to take me into the hospital, for my life was in serious danger. My memories of that time have faded, and all I can say was that I felt like a ghost. I was so light, so pale, so cold, and the hospital didn't sound bad at all, for I had lost all the strength and want to keep myself alive. I just wanted to sleep forever.

My doctors decided that it would be good for me to share a room with Laura, a forty year old cancer patient who didn't have much time left. By doing that, I would have to realize that I caused all this misery myself and that I shouldn't be so ungrateful, since so many people like this woman were trying so hard to have just a few months extra to live. Little did the doctors know that it was just my guilt over my ungratefulness for life that took the shape of a downward spiral. I knew how much my parents were suffering. I knew how much money I had cost the medical institutions, but what I didn't know was how to live. Laura was very kind to me. She knew what was wrong with me and never blamed me for making myself sick. Instead, she showed me that even in the hospital, having fun with little things is what makes fighting for your life worthwhile. I would race her in her wheelchair through the halls of the hospital, speeding past the shouting nurses. We would play card games with a demented woman across our room and we would watch our favorite soap series "As the World Turns" together.

The fluid that was fed through a hose from my nose to my stomach made me feel stronger every day. I had seen the dark side of my own mind, but the continuous efforts and love from my family made me realize that even if I didn't want to live for my own happiness, I still could make other people happy just by getting better. It took me a month in the hospital and years of therapy, but I made it. I blossomed a bit later than other girls, I wore the scars of my disease, but I grew up to be a confident, talkative and motivated young woman. I took up snowboarding and karate, I went hiking in the mountains with my brother, and I devoted a lot of time in partying, taming my bird Valskuiken and reading. Looking back at that time, I think that my disease has in many ways been a blessing to my life, and that without it I wouldn't have seen the beauty of the simple things in life as much as I do now.

Ten years after my hospitalization I found myself eating a hamburger in the cantina of my university in San Francisco. As soon as I caught myself envying the blonde cheerleaders, I smiled at myself and giggled out loud at my own silly happiness. I wrapped up my stuff and headed for a quick toilet break. Sitting down on the paper covers that are available in every American toilet, which I love, I heard the voices of the two cheerleaders coming in. They entered the toilets on either sides of mine and I remember looking at their shoes and thinking it odd that they were turned towards the porcelain, instead of away from it. Until I heard them vomiting. The cheerleaders that I had admired so much only minutes earlier were bulimics. I felt myself nailed to the toilet and when I heard them coming out, one girl asked the other whether she got it all out. I could not believe it. Like me ten years earlier, these girls had an eating disorder, but unlike me, they felt fine with it. It made me sad to think that this must not be uncommon in western consumer societies these days, and there and then on the toilet, I started crying out of pity for the girl that I once was, but just couldn't understand anymore.

The months of my first semester flew by as I was having more and more fun every day. I surrounded myself with a tiny, but great, group of people that I trusted and together we ventured out on drunken evenings, lazy sunny days and stressful hasty coffees at university. My classes were heavy and the workload was incredible to my standards, but I worked hard every day and passed every one of them with an A. By having a Fulbright status I felt the pleasant burden of expectations resting on my shoulders and I was sure to show everybody that their trust in me was not in vain. I have always had the dream of becoming a successful academic one day, and now I knew I would be. Even more than the pride of my Fulbright scholarship, I wanted to show my family my gratitude for their endless love and efforts during all these years of depression I caused them. Before I tried to give them presents and write them little notes, but when I saw the look on my parent's faces as I danced around the room. I noticed that my happiness was their biggest reward.

For the Christmas holiday, Alex and I decided we would spend two weeks with my family and friends in the Netherlands. We left on Christmas day, since the tickets were almost half the price on that day. The flight back "home" brought a mixture of emotions with it. I felt excited to see everybody again, and afraid that I would get homesick again when I had to leave. Holland was all that and more. Seeing my mother, father, brother and sister again felt like a warm bath and it was funny how having them around seemed to be normal again. Seeing my friends was confusing. I was very disappointed that some of the people, whom I considered to be my very best friends, didn't make much of an effort to see me, with excuses ranging from being too tired to too hung-over or simply too busy. Other people however, from whom I never expected it, decided to go out of their way to make sure that they could see me. It has left me confused and wondering about the meaning and expectations of friendships, but at least I do not question my own character anymore. Two weeks in my home country seemed like only two minutes, and the time to say goodbye again came too fast. Like the first time, I made sure not to cry in front of my parents, to show them my courage and strength. Like the first time, I broke down in my boyfriend's arms as soon as we were away from my parents' sight. But it was okay now. I knew I was going back to my second home and my second life in San Francisco, where a new semester and new opportunities awaited me.

Anouk@sfsu.edu

The Contributors

Eric S. Howard (Introduction)
ehoward@FulbrightAcademy.org

Mr. Eric Howard is one of the founders of the Fulbright Academy and serves as its Executive Director. He has been building bridges between people interested in science, technology and business for more than ten years. He was awarded a Fulbright Scholarship to West Germany in 1989 to conduct research at the University of Bonn in land planning, forest management and rural economic development. He also has held fellowships at World Wildlife Fund and at the US Environmental Protection Agency. He earned a B.A. with Honors in Geology from Wesleyan University and a Master of Environmental Management degree with a focus on resource economics and policy from the Nicholas School of the Environment at Duke University. Mr. Howard started his professional career as the Information Officer for the World Conservation Unions Environmental Law Center in Bonn Germany, where he was responsible for collecting and disseminating information on legal and policy developments during the two years leading up to the 1992 Earth Summit in Rio. He has worked as a consultant with the United Nations Environment Program, the US Agency for International Development, as well as national and local organizations. More recently he has been directing non-profit organizations and managing programs with a focus on environmental conservation and science and technology innovation. His written work includes serving as co-editor of The Sourcebook for Conservation and Biological Diversity Information (1995), and as a contributor to the Yearbook of International Environmental Law from 1990-1997.

Alessandra Seggi – Italy
aleseggi@fulbrightweb.org

Alessandra holds a Master's of Art in Media Studies. She is currently pursuing her Ph.D. in Sociology of Media and teaching Italian Language and Film at The New School, in New York. Her interests include languages, Sociolinguistics, Sociology of Film, and Sociology of Mental Health. She was awarded the Fulbright Scholarship in 1999.

Winnie Tarinyeba - Uganda
winta4@yahoo.com

Winnie Tarinyeba hails from Bushenyi in Western Uganda. She is 29 years old and is currently pursuing his graduate studies at the Stanford Law School. Her field of interest is Corporate Governance and Securities Regulation. She is an Assistant Lecturer at the Faculty of Law Makerere University Uganda. She was awarded the Fulbright scholarship in 2005. She has authored many articles on regulation of capital markets. She is a member of the Uganda Law Society and Institute of Corporate Governance.

Zeeshan-ul-hassan Usmani – Pakistan
zeeshan_ul_hassan@yahoo.com

Zeeshan ul-hassan Usmani hails from Sukkur, a small town in Pakistan. He is 27 years old and is currently pursuing his graduate studies at the Florida Institute of Technology in Computer Sciences. His field of interest is swarm intelligence, self-organization and complex systems. He was awarded the Fulbright scholarship in 2004. Zeeshan has authored many articles and two books entitled C/C++ and USA: My Fulbright experience published in 2001 and 2005, respectively. He is also a member of IEEE, ACM and a chartered member of the British Computer Society.

Raymund Espinosa Narag – Philippines
naragray@msu.edu

Raymund Espinosa Narag – 31, was born in Manila – Philippines. He studied in Cagayan National High School, and graduated from University of Philippines. He came to US in Fall 2005 and joined Michigan East University, East Lansing, Michigan.

Marina Lukanina – Russia
moosehead_marina@yahoo.com

Marine is from Moscow, Russia. I graduated from school-studio (University) by Moscow Art Theater majoring in theater management. I got my Fulbright scholarship in 2005 to do my masters in youth arts development. My main interest is camp management. I would like to be a camp director someday and either run my own arts camp or work for someone who has one. My other interests include foreign languages, traveling, and arts.

Louis-Marie Ngamassi Tchouakeu – Cameroon
ngamassi@yahoo.fr

Louis-Marie Ngamassi Tchouakeu was born on May 10 1958, in Banka a village of the Western Province of Cameroon. His is currently The Chief of Service of Planning and Statistics at the University of Dschang, one of the six State owned universities in Cameroon. His field of interest is Information Systems and Information and Communication Technologies for Development (ICT4D). He was awarded the Fulbright Scholarship in 2002 for a master's degree in Information Systems. In 2004 he got the United Nations Fulbright Fellowship for a six-month academic training at the United Nations Economic Commission for Africa in Addis Ababa, Ethiopia.

Lynette J. Chua – Malaysia
lynette.chua@gmail.com

Lynette Chua is a Ph.D. student in Jurisprudence & Social Policy at the University of California-Berkeley. Lynette, who holds a 2005 Malaysian Fulbright scholarship, was born and raised in Malaysia. She spent her undergraduate years at the E.W. Scripps School of Journalism, Ohio University, and worked as a journalist in Tennessee. She subsequently studied law at the National University of Singapore and worked in Singapore. In her doctoral program at Berkeley, Lynette is interested in the relationships among gender, social movements, law and society. She intends to teach, write and conduct research at an academic institution either in law or the social sciences with a focus on gender, law and society.

Katja Ziehmayer – Austria
kcziehmayer@yahoo.com

Katja Ziehmayer was born and raised in Vienna, Austria. She graduated from the University of Vienna with a degree in History and English Language and Literature. In 2003, Katja moved to New Haven, CT to pursue graduate studies in Industrial/Organizational

Psychology on a Fulbright grant. She is currently working in Risk Management for the Knox County Government in Knoxville, Tennessee. Katja has just started work on her first novel and is looking forward to returning to Vienna with her boyfriend and their two cats.

Anouk Bachman – The Netherlands
Anouk@sfsu.edu

    Anouk Bachman was born in 1981 in Breda, a city near the border of The Netherlands and Belgium. She moved to Amsterdam when she was 19 to study Film Studies at the University of Amsterdam, but soon switched to the field of New Media Studies. Her Bachelor's thesis dealt with video game players' identification processes with anthropomorphic animal characters in games. Today Anouk is a Fulbright graduate student in the Humanities at San Francisco State University, where she seeks to bridge the gap between cultural studies, philosophy and video game studies. She is also an editor for an online games magazine and regularly presents her work at conferences.

The Editors

Zeeshan-ul-hassan Usmani
zeeshan_ul_hassan@yahoo.com

Zeeshan ul-hassan Usmani hails from Sukkur, a small town in Pakistan. He is 27 years old and is currently pursuing his graduate studies at the Florida Institute of Technology in Computer Sciences. His field of interest is swarm intelligence, self-organization and complex systems. He was awarded the Fulbright scholarship in 2004. Zeeshan has authored many articles and two books entitled C/C++ and USA: My Fulbright experience published in 2001 and 2005, respectively. He is also a member of IEEE, ACM and a chartered member of the British Computer Society.

Omer Idrees
Omer.idrees@gmail.com

Omer Idrees was described by his sociology teacher as a walking, talking sociology lab. Born and raised in Saudi Arabia, Omer is a Pakistani by decent and is fluent in Arabic, English and Urdu. He picked up Arabic as a child and honed his linguistic skills on the streets of Jeddah during his many escapades involving the game of soccer. He was initially home schooled and was later enrolled in the American school of Jeddah, and so an American undergraduate education seemed like a logical choice. He graduated *cum laude* from the Florida Institute of Technology with a double Bachelor: Electrical Engineering and Computer Engineering. He is currently in the process of setting up his own Engineering Services Company in Jeddah, Saudi Arabia in conjunction with his father, Kunwar Muhammed Idrees.

CPSIA information can be obtained
at www.ICGtesting.com
Printed in the USA
FSOW01n1441040515
6904FS